# THE SHA~~...~~
## OF THE AM~~...~~

**BENJAMIN FRANKLIN** weighing the pros and cons of slavery in terms of pure economics.

**GEORGE WASHINGTON** reluctantly allowing black soldiers into the Continental Army.

**THOMAS JEFFERSON** discussing his view of natural Negro inferiority.

**JAMES MADISON** examining the feasibility of sending all Negroes back to Africa.

*All are part of a history seldom taught in our classrooms. Yet it is a history whose meaning is vital. Only by facing up to the sometimes troubling lessons of our past can we understand the complex problems of the present—and the way to a better future.*

*ABOUT THE AUTHOR:* Matthew T. Mellon was born in Pittsburgh in 1890, received his B.A. at Princeton, his M.A. at Harvard, and his Ph.D. in American History at Albert Ludwig University in Germany. He was a lecturer at the Faculty of Philosophy at the latter university, his fields being English and American literature as well as history.

*ABOUT RICHARD B. MORRIS:* Gouverneur Morris Professor of History at Columbia University, Richard Morris has been editor of the John Jay and Alexander Hamilton papers. His many published works include the forty-volume *Encyclopedia of American History* (with Henry S. Commager), *The Age of Washington, The American Revolution, The Peacemakers* (winner of the Bancroft Prize), and *Basic Documents in American History*.

# SIGNET and MENTOR Books of Related Interest

☐ **THE CONFESSIONS OF NAT TURNER by William Styron.** The record-breaking bestseller and Pulitzer Prize-winning novel about the devoutly religious, well-educated Negro preacher who led a violent revolt against slavery.   (#Y3596—$1.25)

☐ **NARRATIVE OF THE LIFE OF FREDERICK DOUGLASS, AN AMERICAN SLAVE, written by Himself.** With a Preface by William Lloyd Garrison. In the tradition of the bestselling THE CONFESSIONS OF NAT TURNER, an escaped slave who organized an insurrection and lived to tell the world his harrowing story boldly discloses the nightmare world of the pre-Civil War slave in the South.
(#D3434—50¢)

☐ **UNCLE TOM'S CHILDREN by Richard Wright.** Searing short stories highlighting the Negro's desperate fight for survival in the Deep South, by one of our greatest Negro writers, author of BLACK BOY.   (#T3681—75¢)

☐ **CHRONICLES OF BLACK PROTEST edited by Bradford Chambers.** A superlative documentary on Black Power from the pens of Booker T. Washington, Stokely Carmichael, Malcolm X, Martin Luther King, Nat Turner, etc.   (#MQ907—95¢)

☐ **BLACK VOICES: AN ANTHOLOGY OF AFRO-AMERICAN LITERATURE edited by Abraham Chapman.** An exciting and varied anthology of fiction, autobiography, poetry and literary criticism by America's Black writers, among them Ralph Ellison, Richard Wright, and James Baldwin.
(#MW866—$1.50)

---

**THE NEW AMERICAN LIBRARY, INC., P.O. Box 2310, Grand Central Station, New York, New York 10017**

Please send me the SIGNET BOOKS I have checked above. I am enclosing $_____ (check or money order—no currency or C.O.D.'s). Please include the list price plus 10¢ a copy to cover mailing costs. (New York City residents add 5% Sales Tax. Other New York State residents add 2% plus any local sales or use taxes).

Name_____

Address_____

City_____State_____Zip Code_____
Allow at least 3 weeks for delivery

# Early American Views
## on
# NEGRO SLAVERY

*From the Letters and Papers*
*of the Founders of the Republic*

by MATTHEW T. MELLON

*With a New Introduction by RICHARD B. MORRIS*
GOUVERNEUR MORRIS PROFESSOR OF HISTORY,
COLUMBIA UNIVERSITY

A MENTOR BOOK

Published by
THE NEW AMERICAN LIBRARY, New York and Toronto
The New English Library Limited, London

FIRST EDITION PUBLISHED: BOSTON, 1934
NEW EDITION WITH INTRODUCTION BY R. B. MORRIS

© COPYRIGHT, 1969, BY BERGMAN PUBLISHERS, NEW YORK

*All rights reserved. For information address Bergman Publishers,
224 West 20th Street, New York, New York 10011.*

Library of Congress Catalog Card Number: 69-17561

This is an authorized reprint of a hardcover edition published
by Bergman Publishers.

MENTOR TRADEMARK REG. U.S. PAT. OFF. AND FOREIGN COUNTRIES
REGISTERED TRADEMARK—MARCA REGISTRADA
HECHO EN CHICAGO, U.S.A.

MENTOR BOOKS are published *in the United States by*
The New American Library, Inc.,
1301 Avenue of the Americas, New York, New York 10019,
*in Canada* by The New American Library of Canada Limited,
295 King Street East, Toronto 2, Ontario,
*in the United Kingdom* by The New English Library Limited,
Barnard's Inn, Holborn, London, E.C. 1, England

FIRST PRINTING, MAY, 1969

PRINTED IN THE UNITED STATES OF AMERICA

# Introduction

Mr. Mellon's illuminating presentation of the views of some of the Founding Fathers on slavery and the Negro exposes the raw nerve of American democratic society. If the central theme of the American Revolution was freedom and equality, the impact of that epochal struggle upon the black man was at best peripheral. The Declaration of Independence had dedicated the Revolution to the proposition that "all men are created equal." There were some who wondered whether that proposition would be applied to the ending of slavery, the greatest of all human inequalities.

Hardly a month after the Declaration had been adopted, the Patriot Henry Laurens, a South Carolina planter and ex-slave trader, asserted in a letter to his son John his readiness to apply the ideals of the Declaration to the bondsmen of his estates. He planned to manumit them, even though he was opposed by "great powers," as he expressed it, "the laws and customs of my country, my own and the avarice of my countreymen." Laurens denied that he was "one of those who dare trust in providence for defence and security of their own liberty while they enslave and wish to continue in slavery thousands who are as well entitled to freedom as themselves." The fact is, however, that Henry and John Laurens were most exceptional among South Carolinians, for in the Lower

South concern about the slaves was largely confined to expressions of fear that a breakdown on law and order would encourage slave insurrections or that British military advances would prompt slaves to rally to the Redcoat ranks.

What Mr. Mellon has provided for the reader in meticulous detail is a blow-by-blow account of the evolution of the views on slavery and the Negro question held by Benjamin Franklin, John Adams, George Washington, Thomas Jefferson, and James Madison. As might be expected, all five, products of the Enlightenment, are critical of slavery, but the two Northerners, Franklin and Adams, were prepared to strike against the slave system directly and to associate themselves with the movements for manumission while the Southerners, regardless of their humane impulses, felt constrained by the social prejudices of the society in which they dwelled.

To judge the Founding Fathers in terms of the anthropological and sociological concepts of our own time would not only be unfair to them but would constitute a disservice to the cause of history. One cannot leave these quotations stark and unexplained, therefore. One must consider that these liberal-minded statesmen were the products of their own time. What is important is not what they *should* have thought had they the insights which have come out of the modern behavioral sciences, but what they *did* think and *do* in terms of the climate or opinion of their own time.

The settlers who came to America brought with them ingrained race prejudice. Even such reformers as Sir Thomas More and Martin Luther believed that slavery was a necessary social institution. Statesmen and the common man shared the ethnocentric view that the earth belonged to the Christian peoples, who could dispose of the less fortunate non-Christian populations as they saw fit. On the eve of colonization there was a growing awareness of racial differences, and early in the sixteenth century the term "race" came into use in the countries of western and southern Europe. One need not belabor the point that the English seemed more deep-rooted in their prejudice against Negroes and Indians than the Portuguese and Spaniards. The fact is that there was intense prejudice, that prejudice led to discrimination, and discrimination to slavery. If the white man held the African Negro to be an inferior being, that rather widespread and fixed conviction was rooted in no small measure in the enormous cultural gulf between Africa's West Coast Negroes speaking a gullah dialect, lacking a written civilization, and bereft of the saving grace of Christianity.

Winthrop Jordan in *Black Over White*, his monumental treatise on the origins of racial prejudice in America, has underscored what seemed to be the most arresting characteristic of the African—his color. In the course of time black and white came to be polarized, the latter connoting sin, the former virginity; white representing beauty, black ugliness. Much stress was laid, too, among Englishmen on the alleged sexual potency of African males, while the heathen culture of the transported African continued to be measured with an English yardstick.

What, then, is particularly significant about the attitude of our Founding Fathers to the Negro is not the conviction they shared with their white contemporaries in America as to the Negro's inferiority, but rather their general aversion to the system of slavery and their expectation that the system would somehow be alleviated if not eradicated. That they were not activists on behalf of emancipation can be explained by their overriding commitment to the cause of Union and their concern lest anti-slavery agitation would alarm the Lower South and keep that region from making a firm commitment to the government under the new Constitution.

Jefferson, the author of the Declaration of Independence, has been a long-standing target of egalitarians for his alleged inconsistency on the subject of the Negro and slavery. The facts are that Jefferson did as much, if not more, than any of the Founding Fathers to curtail the system of slavery. The clause he inserted in the Great Declaration censuring the slave trade was stricken out by the Congress. His far-reaching proposal in his Ordinance of 1784 to bar slavery from all the western territories after 1800 might well, if adopted, have obviated the coming of the Civil War. And, it must be added, it was Jefferson who affixed his signature to the act of Congress abolishing the slave trade.

Mr. Mellon's analysis of James Madison's views serves to highlight the general consensus of leading statesmen that America could not exist as a biracial society. Hence, Madison coupled his solicitude for the freed Negro with his ardent advocacy of the transportation to aid colonization of ex-slaves in Africa. The colonization movement which the early Presidents sponsored is less important for the minimal results it achieved than for the negative attitude toward racial integration in America which it exemplified. While the proposal to buttress the shaky fortunes of the American Colonization Society with federal funds appealed to a wide sector of public opinion, Congressional representatives from the Cotton States deemed colonization to pose an inherent threat to the survival as well as to the extension of slavery. They managed to block all such appropriation bills. To compound the difficulties of the colonizationists, the rising abolitionist movement denounced colonization as a snare and deception designed to perpetuate the institution of slavery in America by drawing off free Negroes from the population.

One cannot leave Mr. Mellon's account of the Founding Fathers and slavery without pointing out how much more balanced a picture he could have drawn had he included George Mason, Virginia's Revolutionary statesman, and John Jay, New York's great diplomat and jurist, and had he enlarged somewhat upon the ideas of John Adams (so cursorily treated herein), as well as other members of the Adams family.

Author of the Declaration of Rights and of the major part of the constitution of Virginia, Mason was a consistent opponent of the institution of slavery. It was he, a Southerner and large plantation owner, who voiced at the Constitutional Convention the most savage indictment of slavery of any of the Founding Fathers, and at the Virginia ratifying convention it was he who denominated the trade in slaves as "diabolical in itself and disgraceful to mankind."

When Secretary of Foreign Affairs in the Confederation, John Jay wrote the Reverend Richard Price:

> That Men should pray and fight for their own Freedom and yet keep others in Slavery is certainly acting a very inconsistent as well as unjust and perhaps impious part, but the History of Mankind is filled with Instances of human Improprieties.

Again, to another correspondent, he commented, "It is much to be wished that slavery be abolished. The honour of the States, as well as justice and humanity, in my opinion, loudly call upon them to emancipate these unhappy people. To contend for our own liberty, and to deny that blessing to others, involves an inconsistency not to be excused." Not only did he criticize the European powers for their "unmerited oppression" of the peoples of India and Africa, but he conceded that the record of the United States "was far from being irreproachable in this respect," and that it was "very inconsistent with their declarations on the subject of human rights to permit a single slave to be found within their jurisdiction."

As President of the New York Society for Promoting the Manumission of Slaves, Jay drew up a draft memorial to the New York legislature in 1786 to prohibit the exportation of Negroes, and as governor of the state of New York he had the satisfaction of affixing his signature to a bill providing for the gradual emancipation of Negro slaves. In other respects Jay took a more advanced position than Madison, for instance. He believed that every effort should be made by welfare and education to train freedmen to become "useful members of society." In other words, he foresaw a biracial society based on complete equality. As early as 1785 Jay declared:

> I wish to see all unjust and unnecessary discriminations everywhere abolished, and that the time may soon come, when all our inhabitants, of every COLOR and denomination, shall be free and EQUAL PARTAKERS OF OUR POLITICAL LIBERTY.

Verily, Jay, the Founding Father, anticipated the objectives of the Kennedy-Johnson years!

Finally, one cannot leave Mr. Mellon's account of the Founding Fathers and slavery without some further comment on the role of John Adams and his son, John Quincy. The elder Adams authored the Constitution of 1780, whose preamble was quickly interpreted by the courts of Massachusetts Bay as liberating all slaves in that state. An outspoken man, he had been quickly labeled by delegates from the Lower South as an opponent of the slave trade and one not likely to press the claims of the Southern planters for the recovery of slaves taken by British arms. John's wife Abigail was even less equivocal' than her husband on the subject of slaves. Writing to her husband on September 22, 1774, she remarked, "I wish most sincerely there was not a Slave in the province. It allways appeared a most iniquitous Scheme to me — fight ourselfs for what we are daily robbing and plundering from those who have as good a right to freedom as we have. You know my mind upon this Subject."

In a time of great orators John Quincy Adams' generation conferred upon him the title of "the old man eloquent." Most of his fire and invective was reserved for the system of slavery. After leaving the Presidency and coming to Congress as a Representative, John Quincy Adams in the first weeks of his first session presented a batch of petitions on slavery. Devoting the remainder of his life to opposing the extension of slavery to newly acquired territories, he acted as a spearhead for the burgeoning movement to deluge Congress with anti-slavery petitions. In 1836 Congress ruled that no such petitions should be read, printed, committed, or in any way acted upon by the

House, but be laid upon the table without debate or discussion. Each year, from 1836 to 1844, Adams opposed this "gag rule" as a direct violation of the Constitution, and, at the end of 1844 he enjoyed the triumph of seeing the "gag" resolution at last defeated. Although he was the channel for antislavery petitions, he himself was not an abolitionist. Nevertheless, he continued to insist that slavery and democracy were "incompatible." His position was thoroughly consistent with the views of his father, with John Jay, and with other Founding Fathers like Alexander Hamilton, who in the post-revolutionary period was active, along with Jay, in the organization and operation of the New York Society for Promoting the Manumission of Slaves.

Without detracting from the illumination that Mr. Mellon has shed on the views of some of the Founding Fathers, it must be said in conclusion that the case against slavery and for equal treatment of the Negro was more eloquently and effectively presented by other contemporaries whom Mr. Mellon has not chosen to consider, and that race attitudes have over the generations undergone a radical transformation in America, one which few of the Founding Fathers could be expected to anticipate despite their humane feeling and the strong tug of conscience.

Nevertheless, Matthew Mellon must be considered a pioneer in his explanation of the racial attitudes of early American statesmen. Writing as he did in the 1930's, when there was a trend toward hypercritical reassessment of the roots of the American tradition, Mr. Mellon reflected the disillusionment of his generation. At the same time he placed the focus of his research upon the subjects of slavery and race, subjects which had been shunted into a dark corner of the historical record. For the pitiless illumination which he has shed upon these controversial topics and the thoroughness and candor of his analysis, present-day readers will be very much in his debt. If we today are properly concerned about the obstacles in the way of creating a biracial society—obstacles raised by peoples of both races—it will be a source of valuable instruction for all Americans to realize how racial attitudes have evolved from the founding of our republic, and how widespread and pervasive have been the symptoms of race prejudice.

RICHARD B. MORRIS

*Columbia University*

# Contents

## Part III:
## JOHN ADAM'S
## VIEWS ON NEGRO SLAVERY

## Part IV:
## THOMAS JEFFERSON'S
## VIEWS ON NEGRO SLAVERY

## Part V:
## JAMES MADISON'S
## VIEWS ON NEGRO SLAVERY

Early American Views
on
NEGRO SLAVERY

# Preface

The aim of this work has been to show the views of the most important early American statesmen on Negro slavery and the slave trade. The period which I have treated falls between the Revolution and the year 1830. The views considered are those of Benjamin Franklin and the first four presidents of the United States. While it is true that there were others whose views deserve consideration, it will be found, I am convinced, that the men whom I have selected were the true leaders in the development of early thought on the Negro problem. Because of their political prominence they were in correspondence with other important leaders, and thus the views of men such as Alexander Hamilton, General Lafayette and others have found their way into the text.

So that the reader might be in a position to form his own opinions, I have, wherever possible, allowed the authors to speak for themselves through the medium of their own writings. Care has also been taken to present the material against a general historical background so that foreigners and others not well acquainted with American history might be spared the trouble of much reading.

I would like to point out for the benefit of the reader who wishes to arrive at the essence of this book without too much effort, that I have prepared a summary of each man's views at the end of the section bearing his name. I have also placed at the very end of the book some general conclusions to which the whole study of the problem has lead me.

MATTHEW T. MELLON

Hyannis, Mass.
June, 1934

## PART I

# Benjamin Franklin's Views on Negro Slavery

## I.

### Franklin's Education and Early Environment

In treating of Franklin's views on Negro slavery it is important to bear in mind that his long life and writings fall mostly before the time of the American Revolution. He was twenty-six years older than Washington and thirty-seven years older than Jefferson, so that at the time of the Revolution Franklin was looked upon as an older man, whose opinions were of great value. That his advice was eagerly sought, is proved by his appointment to the committee which penned the Declaration of Independence; and by the active part he took in the congressional debates in which the American Constitution was shaped.

Born in Boston in 1706, fifteenth in a family of seventeen of a poor candle-maker and soap-boiler who had migrated from England, Franklin's youth was devoid of luxuries and comforts known to Washington and Jefferson. There were no Negro slaves or servants in his father's household and there is no evidence that young Franklin came into contact with Negroes in any way, for there were very few of them at that time in all New England, and these were mostly employed as servants in the houses of the rich.

The New England of his day was just emerging

5

out of the mediaevalism which the theology of Calvin
had imposed upon it under the Mather dynasty. Only
fourteen years before Franklin's birth, both Increase
and Cotton Mather had sanctioned the sentence of
some nineteen persons who were hanged for witch-
craft. When the people began slowly to regain their
senses and to realize the danger of the religious hys-
teria into which their pastors had led them, the end
of church domination had begun. Besides this the
Colonists were tired of the pessimism which Puritan
theology imposed upon them. The material opportunities which America offered made men doubtful
whether the world were such a vale of tears as the
church made it out to be. Thus the religion of the
"agonized conscience" gradually gave way to that of
good will among men, and it was at the dawn of this
new liberalism that Franklin was born. That he became responsible in no small way for this change;
that his own example and writings left their imprint
upon Americans, not only of the eighteenth century,
but of the nineteenth and twentieth as well, is recognized.

Franklin began life by being baptized in the Old
South Church in Boston. At the age of eight he was
sent to grammar school. At this time, it appears, his
father intended to educate him for the ministry. But,
a year later he was sent to a private school to learn
writing and arithmetic. After two years there, he was
apprenticed into his father's business, which didn't
appeal to the boy. To avoid the possibility of the
boy's running away to sea, his father apprenticed him
to his half-brother, James, a printer, who was the publisher of Boston's most liberal newspaper, "The New
England Courant." This paper was often at odds
with the Puritan authorities and during such times

as his brother was forced to spend in jail, young Franklin took over the paper with such success that the older brother became jealous of Franklin's ability. After five years of quarreling with James, Franklin left Boston in the fall of 1723 for Philadelphia, where with the exception of the years he spent in England and France, he lived until his death in 1790.

There is no place here to recount the various incidents of Franklin's early life. He, himself, has done it so well in his famous "Autobiography" as to make future biographies superfluous. I wish only to indicate as briefly as possible a few of the most important facts which throw light upon his later life. His work on the newspaper was an experience which gave a liberal turn to his thoughts. Here he was always in the midst of political and intellectual strife which awakened in him the desire to think for himself and not confuse authority with truth.

The books which young Franklin read give us another clue to the way in which his later life shaped itself. Among the usual books in the library of Puritan families, such as the King James Bible, Bunyan's "Pilgrim's Progress" and various works by the Reverend Cotton Mather, there were Plutarch's "Lives," Defoe's "Essays," Locke's "Treatise" and the third volume of Addison and Steele's "Spectator." This last book had a tremendous effect upon Franklin's literary style, and through it the boy developed a love for the chatty, witty life of the London coffeehouses, a love which never forsook him. The knack of drawing a moral from the slightest happening in everyday life was another trait which he learned from Addison. It was due rather to his reading and his own efforts towards self-education, rather than to schools, that Franklin made headway. And it was by his extolling the virtues of commonsense, thrift and making a success in the world (which meant, making money), that he endeared himself to the middle classes in America and has served them ever since as their model. The great danger for most men who are guided by commonsense is that they usually turn out to be commonplace. Franklin was an exception. He first introduced wit and humor into American letters and brought them into contact with the English literature of the same period. He fought the theological writers who had hitherto been holding the field, especially in New England. It is not without reason that he has been called "The Father of the Yankees."

## II.

### Colonial Views on Slavery

Although Franklin dabbled in nearly every problem of his day, from scientific research to political economy and morals, and although he made occasional important contributions to some of them, the fact remains that not until well after middle life did he take any active interest in the problems connected with Negro slavery. It was only in the last few years of his life, when he held the position of president of the Pennsylvania Abolition Society, that he really began to realize the evils of the system and to take definite action against them.

The reason for this was perhaps the general impression, held in the South as well as in the North, that slavery was only a temporary institution. The moral principles involved were not debated because no one attempted to defend slavery openly as a righteous or moral institution. Again, it was thought to be a man's privilege to own slaves or not, as he saw fit. The principle of individual liberty and the slow growth of the idea of moral responsibility were also factors. In early colonial times there were slaves in every colony, but the general opinion was that it was a necessary evil which would not last long. Besides this, the early settlers, particularly in New England, were far too busy looking after the salvation of their own souls to worry much about the souls of others.

Among the reasons why slavery was looked upon as a temporary, rather than a permanent, institution, was that while slaves could be employed with profit in clearing away the forests, they were too expensive to use in general farming or as laborers in factories. In the following quotation we find Franklin quieting the fears of British manufacturers as to possible future competition of American slave labor.

*"Observations Concerning the Increase of Mankind and the Peopling of Countries. Written in Pennsylvania, 1751"*

"It is an ill-grounded opinion that, by the labor of slaves, America may possibly vie in cheapness of manufactures with Britain. The labor of slaves can never be so cheap here as the labor of workingmen is in Britain. Any one may compute it. Interest of money is in the Colonies from six to ten percent. Slaves, one with another, cost thirty pounds sterling per head. Reckon then the interest of the first purchase of a slave, the insurance or risk on his life, his clothing and diet, expenses in his sickness and loss of time, loss by his neglect of business (neglect is natural to the man who is not to be benefited by his own care or diligence), expense of a driver to keep him at work, and his pilfering from time to time, almost every slave being by nature a thief, and compare the whole amount with the wages of a manufacturer of iron or wool in England, you will see that labor is much cheaper there than it ever can be by Negroes here. Why then will Americans purchase slaves? Because slaves may be kept as long as a man pleases, or has occasion for their labor; while hired men are continually leaving their masters (often in the midst of his business) and setting up for themselves."[1]

Although Franklin was forty-five years old when the above pamphlet was written, it is, nevertheless, the first allusion to the Negroes to be found in his collected letters and writings. He appears interested only in the economics of slavery and entertains a rather low opinion of Negro character. He seems to attribute their thievery much more to their circumstances as slaves, than to any natural flaw in character.

The next allusion in Franklin's works to Negroes occurs some nine years later in a letter to his wife, Deborah, written from London and dated June 27, 1760. The letter reads in part:—

"The paragraph of your letter, inserted in the papers, related to the Negro school. I gave it to the gentleman concerned, as it was a testimony in favor of their pious design. But I did not expect they would print it in your name. They have since chosen me one of the Society, and I am at present chairman for the current year. I enclose you an account of their proceedings."[2]

The actual content of this letter is of little importance. It shows, however, that Franklin was an acting trustee for an English fund to convert Negroes as early as 1760. The Society alluded to in this letter, had been founded by an English philanthropist named Dr. Thomas Bray, who had become acquainted with a rich Dutchman, M. D'Allone, then living at the Hague. M. D'Allone was interested in schemes for converting Negroes and gave Dr. Bray a "considerable sum of money" during his lifetime, for the conversion of Negroes in the British Plantations. When he died he left nine hundred pounds sterling to Dr. Bray for the continuance of the work. Dr. Bray then formed a society for the proper administration of the fund, but after his death in 1730, the work was carried on by a company of gentlemen known as "Dr. Bray's Associates." Franklin, while in England, served for several years as one of these "associates."[3] This appears to be the first time he showed any interest in the Negro race. It is well to note that no effort was made to liberate or educate these unfortunate people, but only to convert them to Christianity and allow them to remain in slavery despite the open conflict with its teaching. It is hard to believe that Franklin, who was a dissenter and Deist, undertook this soul-saving work—as much for his own faith in its necessity, as he did for the position and the respectability which it reflected.

In 1764, Franklin printed a pamphlet in Philadelphia entitled, "A Narrative of the late Massacres in Lancaster Country, etc., etc." This paper contains many anecdotes relating to the Indians and early settlers. Among these anecdotes appears, strangely enough, "an instance of . . . honor in a poor unenlightened African Negro." He tells us how Cudjoe, a poor Negro, saved the life of a white man named William Murry on the coast of Guinea in 1752. Capt. Seagrave, in whose book Franklin read the story, ends the narrative with the remark, "I relate this to show that some of these dark people have a strong sense of justice and honor, and that even the most brutal among them are capable of feeling the force of reason and of being influenced by a fear of God, (if the knowledge of the true God could be introduced among them), since even the fear of a false God, when their rage subsided, was not without its good effect."[4]

The fact that Franklin included this story in his pamphlet, proves that he was becoming interested in Negro character and was beginning to entertain a better opinion of it.

It was not until eight years later that he again concerned himself with Negroes; this time with the slave trade which he calls, "a detestable commerce." Franklin in England and now sixty-six years old wrote the following letter in August of 1772 to his friend, Anthony Benezet, a gentleman born in France who had lived the greater part of his life in Philadelphia, where he belonged to the Society of Friends (Quakers) and interested himself in various forms of philanthropy. Although Benezet gave liberally to all kinds of charities, his main interest was in helping the Negroes and putting an end to the slave trade. He gave not only money to these ends but also is accredited with writing many pamphlets which helped prepare the public sentiment for the ending of this trade in 1808.

"I have made a little extract of yours of April 27th, (wrote Franklin) of the number of slaves imported and perishing with some close remarks on the hypocrisy of this country (England) which encourages such a detestable commerce by laws for promoting the Guinea trade; while it piqued itself on its virtue, love and liberty, and the equity of its courts, in setting free a single Negro. This was inserted in the 'London Chronicle,' of the 20th of June last.

". . . I am glad to hear that the disposition against keeping Negroes grows more general in North America. Several pieces have been lately printed here against the practise, and I hope in time it will be taken into consideration and suppressed by the legislative. Your labors have already been attended with great effects. I hope, therefore, you and your friends will be encouraged to proceed."[5]

The above letter is particularly important because it contains Franklin's first expression of the hope that the trade might be suppressed by law.

It is a fact that as Franklin grew older his interest in broad reforms, and particularly in helping the Negroes, increased. In a letter addressed to Dean Woodward, dated London, April 10th, 1773, Dr. Franklin says:

". . . I have since had the satisfaction to learn that a disposition to abolish slavery prevails in North America; that many of the Pennsylvanians have set their slaves at liberty; and that even the Virginia Assembly have petitioned the king for permission to make a law for preventing the importation of more into that Colony. This request, however, will probably not be granted, as their former laws of that kind have always been repealed, and as the interest of a few merchants here (London) has more weight with the government than that of thousands at a distance."[6]

We find Franklin at the age of sixty-seven expressing satisfaction that a disposition to abolish slavery in North America prevails. It is not until eleven years later that we find another reference to slavery in Franklin's letters. Two Americans, a Mr. Sears and Mr. Smith, had imported a cargo of slaves to the

Island of "Martinico" (probably Martinique) where their cargo was held because the owners refused to pay one hundred livres per head on the Negroes. These gentlemen wrote to Franklin, who was representing the United States at that time in France, asking him to see whether or not this duty could be avoided. Franklin answered from his house in Passy in August of the year 1784:

". . . It cannot be expected that a general national law should be set aside in favor of a particular foreign ship; especially as the King, if he forgives the duty to the stranger, must thereby do injustice to his own subjects, to whom he had promised the produce of that duty, unless he pays it to them out of his own money, which we cannot decently request him to do. I do not, therefore, see any possibility of your avoiding payment."[7]

## III.

### Franklin and the Pennsylvania Abolition Society

It is not my purpose here to give a history of the Pennsylvania Abolition Society but merely a sketch of this remarkable body whose work interested Franklin so much in his old age.

The society was formed before the American Revolution and had the distinction of being the oldest society of its kind in the world. John Baldwin was the first president but the carrying-on of the war so absorbed public interest that most of the work had to be suspended. In 1784, however, the society became very active again. No records were kept of the work accomplished until 1787 when its constitution was changed and Franklin became president. The

name of the society was changed to "the Pennsylvania Society for promoting the abolition of slavery,
the relief of free Negroes unlawfully held in bondage,
and for improving the condition of the African race."
By becoming president of this society, Franklin
showed that he still believed in the doctrine of human
rights and self-evident truths expressed in the Declaration of Independence. This interest in philanthropy
did much to justify his reputation as a great man.

After he had returned from France and had again
taken up residence in Philadelphia, he received a
letter from a friend in London, a Dr. Price, who had
written a pamphlet entitled, "Observations on the
Importance of American Liberty."[1] The letter was
dated September 26, 1787. In it he informed Franklin
what pleasure had been given him to learn that
Franklin's name had been added to the rolls of the
Pennsylvania Society for Abolishing Negro Slavery.
He added:

"A similar institution to yours, for abolishing Negro
slavery, is just formed in London. . . . I need not say
how earnestly I wish success to such institutions.
Something, perhaps, will be done with the view by
the convention of delegates. (The Convention framing
the Constitution of the United States) . . . May God
guide their deliberations. The happiness of the world
depends, in some degree, on the result."

"In this part of the world there is a spirit rising,
which must in time produce great effects."[2] "This
spirit originated in America. . . . The minds of men
are becoming more enlightened; and the silly despots
of the world are likely to be forced to respect human
rights, and to take care not to govern too much, lest
they should not govern at all."[3]

In the fall of 1789, Franklin wrote to "The Pennsylvania Society for Promoting the Abolition of Slavery, and the Relief of Free Negroes Unlawfully Held in Bondage," of which he was then the president, putting before that society a paper entitled, "Plan for Improving the Condition of the Free Blacks."[4]

He recommended that a committee of twenty-four persons should be elected at the next meeting of the society, and that "in order to perform the different services with expedition, regularity, and energy, this committee shall resolve itself into the following sub-committees, viz.

"I. A Committee of Inspection, who shall superintend the morals, general conduct, and ordinary situation of the free Negroes, and afford them advice and instruction, protection from wrongs, and other friendly offices.

"II. A Committee of Guardians, who shall place out children and young people with suitable persons, that they may (during a moderate time of apprenticeship or servitude) learn some trade or other business of subsistence." Another duty of this committee was to secure for the society, "the right of guardianship over the persons so bound."

"III. A Committee of Education, who shall superintend the school instruction of the children and youth of the free blacks." It was to "provide, that the pupils may receive such learning as is necessary for their future situation in life" and to acquaint them with "the most important and generally acknowledged moral and religious principles." Also to keep a record of all the marriages, births and manumissions of all free blacks.

"IV. A Committee of Employ, who shall endeavor

to . . . find common labor for a great number" to avoid "poverty, idleness, and many vicious habits."

These committees should "act in concert" when necessary and "Affairs of great importance" shall be referred to the whole committee. The expenses should be "defrayed by a fund" and this committee of twenty-four should report their progress at the quarterly meetings of the society. Such in brief was the plan.

A few days later Franklin received a letter from a certain John Wright in London, who enclosed the yearly report of a British abolition society in which it was claimed that this society had sown the first seed in the matter of freeing the slaves. Franklin, who was now an old man of eighty-four, was beginning to take a very active interest in the fight for freeing the Negroes. He, accordingly, sat down and wrote the following letter to show that earlier efforts had been made in America.

It reads in part:—

Nov. 4, 1789

". . . I wish success to your endeavors for obtaining an abolition of the slave-trade. The epistle from your yearly Meeting, for the year 1758, was not the first sowing of the good seed you mention; for I find, by an old pamphlet in my possession, that George Keith, near a hundred years since, wrote a paper against the practice, said to be 'given forth by the appointment of the meeting held by him at Philip James house, in the city of Philadelphia, about the year 1693'; wherein a strict charge was given to Friends, 'that they should set their Negroes at liberty, after some reasonable time of service, etc., etc. . . .' And, about the year 1728 or 29, I myself printed a book for Ralph Sandyford, another of your Friends in this city, against keeping Negroes in slavery; two editions of which he distributed gratis. And, about the year 1736, I printed another book on the same subject, for Benjamin Lay, who also professed being one of your Friends; and he distributed the books chiefly among them. By these instances, it appears that the seed was indeed sown in the good ground of your profession, though much earlier than the time you mention; and, its springing up to effect at last, though so late, is some confirmation of Lord Bacon's observation, that a good notion never dies; and it may encourage us in making such, though hopeless of their taking immediate effect."[5]

Only five days later, there appeared in print, "An Address to the Public"; from the above society and signed by its president, the eighty-four year old Franklin.

I quote the entire address:

## An Address to the Public

"From the Pennsylvania Society for Promoting the Abolition of Slavery, and the Relief of Free Negroes unlawfully held in Bondage.

"It is with peculiar satisfaction we assure the friends of humanity, that, in prosecuting the design of our association, our endeavors have proved successful, far beyond our most sanguine expectations.

"Encouraged by this success, and by the daily progress of that luminous and benign spirit of liberty which is diffusing itself throughout the world, and humbly hoping for the continuance of the divine blessing on our labors, we have ventured to make an important addition to our original plan; and do therefore earnestly solicit the support and assistance of all who can feel the tender emotions of sympathy and compassion, or relish the exalted pleasure of benificence.

"Slavery is such an atrocious debasement of human nature, that its very extirpation, if not performed with solicitous care, may sometimes open a source of serious evils.

"The unhappy man, who has long been treated as a brute animal, too frequently sinks beneath the common standard of the human species. The galling chains that bind his body do also fetter his intellectual faculties, and impair the social affections of his heart. Accustomed to move like a mere machine, by the will of a master, reflection is suspended; he has not the power of choice; and reason and conscience have but little influence over his conduct, because he is chiefly governed by the passion of fear. He is poor and friendless; perhaps worn out by extreme labor, age, and disease.

"Under such circumstances, freedom may often prove a misfortune to himself, and prejudicial to society.

"Attention to emancipated black people, it is therefore to be hoped, will become a branch of our national policy; but, as far as we contribute to promote this emancipation, so far that attention is evidently a serious duty encumbent on us, which we mean to discharge to the best of our judgment and abilities.

"To instruct, to advise, to qualify those who have been restored to freedom, for the exercise and enjoyment of civil liberty; to promote in them habits of industry; to furnish them with employments suited to their age, sex, talents, and other circumstances; and to procure their children an education calculated for

their future situation in life,—these are the great out-
lines of the annexed plan, which we have adopted,
and which we conceive will essentially promote the
public good, and the happiness of these our hitherto
too much neglected fellow creatures.

"A plan so extensive cannot be carried into execution without considerable pecuniary resources, beyond
the present ordinary funds of the society. We hope
much from the generosity of enlightened and benevolent freemen, and will gratefully receive any donations
or subscriptions for this purpose which may be made
to our Treasurer, James Stars, or to James Pemberton,
Chairman of our Committee of Correspondence.

"Signed by order of the Society,
"B. FRANKLIN, *President*

"Phila., 9th of November 1789"

## IV.

### Franklin's Memorial to Congress and the Debate that Followed

The last public act of Franklin before his death
was the signing of the following memorial to Congress
on the third of February, 1790. This memorial was
sent to Congress from the Pennsylvania Abolition
Society of which he was president. It read as follows:—

"The memorial respectfully showeth,—

"That, from a regard for the happiness of mankind,
an association was formed several years since in this
state, by a number of her citizens of various religious
denominations, for promoting the abolition of slavery,
and for the relief of those unlawfully held in bondage.
A just and acute conception of the true principles

of liberty, as it spread through the land, produced accessions to their numbers, many friends to their cause, and a legislative co-operation with their views, which, by the blessing of Divine Providence, have been successfully directed to the relieving from bondage a large number of their fellow-creatures of the African race. They have also the satisfaction to observe, that, in consequence of that spirit of philanthropy and genuine liberty which is generally diffusing its beneficial influence, similar institutions are forming at home and abroad.

"That mankind are all formed by the same Almighty Being, alike objects of his care, and equally designed for the enjoyment of happiness, the Christian religion teaches us to believe, and the political creed of Americans fully coincides with the position. Your memorialists, particularly engaged in attending to the distresses arising from slavery, believe it their indispensable duty to present this subject to your notice. They have observed, with real satisfaction, that many important and salutary powers are vested in you for 'promoting the welfare and securing the blessings of liberty to the people of the United States'; and as they conceive that these blessings ought rightfully to be administered, without distinction of color, to all descriptions of people, so they indulge themselves in the pleasing expectation, that nothing which can be done for the relief of the unhappy objects of their care, will be either omitted or delayed.

"From a persuasion that equal liberty was originally the portion, and is still the birth-right, of all men; and influenced by the strong ties of humanity, and the principles of their institution, your memorialists conceive themselves bound to loosen the bands of

slavery, and promote a general enjoyment of the blessings of freedom. Under these impressions, they earnestly entreat your serious attention to the subject of
slavery; that you will be pleased to countenance the
restoration of liberty to those unhappy men, who
alone, in this land of freedom, are degraded to perpetual bondage, and who, amidst the general joy of
surrounding freemen, are groaning in servile subjec-
tion; that you will devise means for removing this inconsistency from the character of the American people; that you will promote mercy and justice toward
this distressed race; and that you will step to the very
verge of the power vested in you for discouraging
every species of traffic in the persons of our fellow-
men.                 "BENJAMIN FRANKLIN, *President*" [1]

Philadelphia, February 3, 1790

Just a day before this memorial reached the House
of Representatives (Feb. 11, 1790), the Quakers (Society of Friends) presented a somewhat similar memorial. This was attacked on the floor as an "intolerant
act of one religious sect to force its own ideas of morality upon the country at large." . . . Mr. Stone of
Maryland declared that it was "unfortunate that religious sects seemed to imagine that they understood
the rights of human nature better than all the world
besides. . . ." [2]

Mr. Jackson of Georgia, who although born in England, had become an officer in the Revolutionary
War on the American side and had even sat in the
Convention which framed the Constitution, wanted
"to know if the whole morality of the world is confined to the Quakers? . . . The Savior had more
benevolence and commiseration than they pretend
to have, and he admitted slavery." [3]

The next day, February 12th, the memorial of the Pennsylvania Abolition Society which Franklin had penned, was presented to the House. Mr. Tucker of South Carolina was "surprised to see another memorial on the same subject, and that signed by a man (Franklin) who ought to have known the Constitution better." [4] He went on to say that the Southern clergy supported slavery, which while true, only shows how weak and futile principles are when confronted with the economic desires of a people.

Mr. Smith of South Carolina declared that the Southern States "would never have entered the Confederation unless their property had been guaranteed to them. . . . When we entered into this Confederacy we did it from political and not from moral motives. And I don't think my constituents want to learn morals from the petitioners. . . . If they do, they can learn it at home." [5]

As the debate was getting onto dangerous ground; ground upon which afterwards was to split the Union, it was referred to a committee. The outcome was that they denied the right of the government to interfere with the slave trade until the year 1808, as decided in the Constitutional Convention. The debate ended on March twenty-third. It distinguished very clearly the differences which were to be emphasized during the next seventy years and which played such a great part in bringing on the Civil War.

President Washington saw the immediate danger and took a rather cool attitude toward the memorialists whom he regarded as annoying disturbers. He was willing to sacrifice a great many of his principles in order to preserve the Union which he had fought so hard to create. In future sessions of Congress when memorials of this nature appeared they simply were put to one side and never referred to again.

Franklin was sensitive to the rebuff his memorial had received in Congress. Only two days passed before the ending of the debate before he sent the following article to the "Federal Gazette" where it appeared in print. This was one of the last things that Franklin ever did, for only twenty days later he died. It is a tribute to his energy and interest in the problem that he could exhibit so much spontaneous wit at this advanced age and in his feeble state of health. The paper is a typical Franklin parody on the arguments used by the men who had defended slavery, particularly Mr. Jackson of Georgia.

I quote it in part:—[6]

"To the Editor of the 'Federal Gazette'

March 23rd, 1790

"Sir,—Reading last night in your excellent paper the speech of Mr. Jackson in Congress against their meddling with the affair of slavery, or attempting to mend the condition of the slaves, it put me in mind of a similar one, made about one hundred years since, by Sidi Mehemet Ibrahim, a member of the Divan of Algiers, which may be seen in Martin's Account on his Consulship, anno 1687. It was against granting the petition of the sect called 'Erika,' or Purists, who prayed for the abolition of piracy and slavery as being unjust. Mr. Jackson does not quote it: perhaps he has not seen it. If, therefore, some of his reasonings are to be found in this eloquent speech, it may only show that men's interests and intellects operate, and are operated on, with surprising similarity in all countries and climates, whenever they are under similar circumstances. The African's speech, as translated, is as follows:—

" 'Allah Bismillah, etc. God is great and Mahomet is his prophet.

" 'Have this Erika considered the consequences of granting their petition? If we cease our cruises against the Christians, how shall we be furnished with the commodities their countries produce, and which are so necessary for us? If we forbear to make slaves of their people, who, in this hot climate, are to cultivate our lands? Must we not then be our own slaves? And is there not more compassion and more favor due us as Mussulmen than to these Christian dogs? . . . And for what? To gratify the whims of a whimsical sect, who would have us not only forbear making more slaves, but even manumit those we have.

" 'But who is to indemnify their masters for the loss? Will the state do it? Is our treasury sufficient? Will the Erica do it? Can they do it? Or would they, to do what they think justice to the slaves, do a greater injustice to the owners? And, if we set our slaves free, what is to be done with them? Few of them will return to their countries; they know too well the greater hardships they must there be subject to; they will not embrace our holy religion; they will not adopt our manners; our people will not pollute themselves by inter-marrying with them. Must we maintain them as beggars in our streets, or suffer our properties to be the prey of their pillage?

" 'The sun of Islamism gives forth its light, and shines in full splendor; and they have an opportunity for making themselves acquainted with the true doctrine, and thereby saving their immortal souls. Those who remain at home have not that happiness. Sending the slaves home, then, would be sending them out of the light into darkness. . . . The condition of most of them is, therefore, already mended, and requires not further improvement. Here their lives are in safety. They are not liable to be impressed for soldiers, and forced to cut one another's Christian throats, as in the wars of their own countries. If some of the religious-mad bigots who tease us with their silly petitions, have, in a fit of blind zeal, freed their slaves, it was not generosity, it was not humanity, that moved them to the action: it was from the conscious burthen of a load of sins, and a hope, from the supposed merits of so good a work, to be excused from damnation.

" 'How grossly are they mistaken to suppose slavery to be disallowed by the Alcoran! Are not the two precepts, to quote no more, "Master, treat your slaves with kindness; slaves, serve your masters with cheerfulness and fidelity," clear proofs to the contrary? Nor can the plundering of infidels be in that sacred book forbidden, since it is well known from it that God has given the world, and all that it contains, to his faithful Mussulmen, who are to enjoy it of right as fast as they conquer it? Let us, then, hear no more of this detestable proposition,—the manumission of Christian slaves; . . . I have, therefore, no doubt but this wise council will prefer the comfort and happiness of a whole nation of true believers to the whim of a few Erika, and dismiss their petition.'

"The result was, as Martin tells us, that the Divan came to this resolution: 'The doctrine that plundering and enslaving the Christians is unjust, is, at best, problematical; but that it is the interest of this state to continue the practice, is clear: therefore let the petition be rejected.'

"And it was rejected accordingly.

"And since like motives are apt to produce in the minds of men like opinions and resolutions, may we not, Mr. Brown, venture to predict, from this account, that the petitions to the parliament of England for abolishing the slave trade, to say nothing of other Legislatures, and the debates upon them, will have a similar conclusion?

"I am, Sir, your constant reader and humble servant.

"HISTORICUS" [7]

## V.

### Summary of Franklin's Views

We have seen that Franklin did not become actively interested in helping the Negroes or in freeing them until late in life. His youth was lived in the North where only a few slaves were used in the houses of the rich. Slavery before the Revolution was thought to be a temporary evil which time would alter and in the absence of a definite pro-slavery party, there was nothing for the reformers to attack. He first became interested in slavery from a purely economic standpoint. In 1751 he showed that Negro slaves could never compete with free, white labor in industry. In 1760 we find him serving as trustee for a British fund to convert Negroes on British Plantations to Christianity. This society was not interested in freeing them. In 1764, Franklin included an account of a good African who had saved the life of a white man in a pamphlet which he wrote. This shows that his opinion of Negro character was improving at this early date. In 1772 he branded the slave trade as "a detestable commerce" in a letter to Anthony Benezet and added that he was "glad to hear that the disposition against keeping Negroes grows more general in North America." He also expressed in the same letter a view which Washington likewise held. "I hope in time it (slavery) will be . . . suppressed by the legislature."

It was the Pennsylvania Abolition Society that first made Franklin really aware of the injustice of slavery. As its president he began to take a very active interest in abolition. He suggested changes in the committee of this society which made its work much more effective. When the Englishman, John Wright, wrote him that the first seed toward abolition had been sown in England, the eighty-four year old Franklin replied with a long letter showing that the Quakers as early as 1693 had shown an interest in freeing the Negroes. Only a few days later in his "An Address To the Public," he called slavery an "atrocious debasement of human nature." His last public act was to pen a memorial to Congress for the Pennsylvania Abolition Society, "for promoting the abolition of slavery, and for the relief of those unlawfully held in bondage." A great debate followed in Congress which lasted nearly a month and in which the first signs of local differences of opinion regarding the institution of slavery became evident.

The last paper, so far as is known, that Franklin ever wrote was a parody upon the arguments which the Southern legislators had used to defend the institution. He showed not only a remarkable zeal for reform in his old age but retained his clear-headedness and wit to the very end.

## PART II

# George Washington's Views on Negro Slavery

(A History of their Development)

## I.

### The Real and False Washington

Up until recently, a great deal of nonsense, inspired by a false national pride, has appeared in America in connection with the life of George Washington. "Parson" Weems, one of the first offenders, seems to have set the mode for the early biographers in his incredible biography entitled "A History of the Life and Death, Virtues and Exploits of General George Washington." In this work he invented incidents, such as the well-known "cherry tree" story, to illustrate the "private virtues" of the great man. On the very first page of the work we find no other than the Emperor Napoleon I exclaiming, "Posterity will talk of him (Washington) with reverence as the founder of a great empire, when my name shall be lost in the Vortex of Revolutions!" The result of the good Parson's work was to take every bit of humanity out of Washington's life and to set him up on so high a pedestal, that generations of Americans could only regard him as a curious heaven-sent phenomenon having very little to do with lowly human beings like themselves. Thus began the Washington myth which made of him a "plaster saint" for millions of American schoolboys to whom criticism of "the father of his country" was little less than treason.

The results of recent research have brought out many facts which demonstrate that George Washington, far from being the "plaster saint" of Parson Weems' biography, was in reality a very human being. When the iconoclasts first showed Washington to be a man of real flesh and blood, who kept over two hundred slaves, drank alcoholic beverages and was suspected of having illicit relations with his slave women, a great cry arose in the land. Patriotic societies, the clergy and other upholders of public morals fought bitterly to preserve the "plaster saint" conception of Washington. But theirs was a losing fight. The result is that a new and more human Washington, a Washington with whom we can sympathize and understand, has emerged from the smoke of the critical battle.

We are concerned here with Washington's views on the subject of Negro slavery. Many biographies of Washington fail to mention the words "Negro" or "slave" and avoid all mention of him as a slaveholder. His life has been treated from nearly every angle; as soldier, statesman, economist and even as country gentleman, but it is as a slave-holder we must study him here. And this is not too small a part of his many-sided life to consider separately. For the development of Washington's views toward the Negro was in a constant process of change throughout his whole life, and it is only by understanding what a tremendous advance he made beyond the views of his fellow slaveholders, that we can rightly appraise his efforts. His ideas of liberty came to him directly from his environment and practical experience; not from books or from the borrowed views of European political philosophers. He

never claimed to be consistent in his views or to have
worked out any logical system of thought. He was not
given much to oratory and often realized that he could
gain more by compromise than by being obstinate. In
other words, there was much of the practical leader
and politician in him with something of a distrust of
theory. He realized that even revolutions cannot
change human beings overnight, and there were times
when he remained strangely silent in the interest of
what he considered more important issues. His interest in purely moral questions was never very great.
That is why he disapproved of slavery more on social
and economic than on moral grounds. But how could
it be otherwise when we consider that Washington
was not only born a slaveholder, but born into an
environment which held that the holding of slaves was
not only a necessity, but also a righteous necessity? In
the Virginia of his day, slavery was not only universal
but also was upheld by the law of the land as well as
by the official sanction of the Church of England. To
understand how Washington's views toward Negro
slavery changed, is to understand the development of
his whole ideas toward liberty and human rights.


## II.

### Slavery and the Virginia Tradition

It is hard for us today who regard slavery as a crime
comparable with rape or felony to understand the
ideas of the eighteenth century plantation owner in
Virginia. In that colony as well as in many others "the
system" was taken as a matter of fact. Washington's
family had been slaveholders for three generations
before his birth and the boy was brought up to accept

the institution as being not only a natural and moral one but a necessary one as well. We do not read of Virginia gentlemen being troubled by their consciences about slavery; the institution was simply taken for granted. Besides this, the Church of England, which was in Washington's youth and had been for a century and a half, the official religion in the colony, supported the institution whole-heartedly. The Colony had a just fear of the Negro population and were always on guard against an insurrection of the blacks. Accordingly the law required that twice a year a proclamation should be read in all the churches of the colony in which it was held unlawful "for any Negro to arm himself with any club, staff, gun, sword or any weapon of defense or offense, or to depart from his master's ground without a pass, to be granted only on particular and necessary occasions." [1]

Thomas Jefferson in his "Notes on Virginia" gives us a short description of the evil influence of slavery upon the youth of the colony.

"The whole commerce between master and slave is a perpetual exercise of the most boisterous passions, the most unremitting despotism on the other. Our children see this, and learn to imitate it; for man is an imitative animal . . . the child . . . puts on the same airs in the circle of smaller slaves . . . and thus nursed, educated, and daily exercised in tyranny, cannot but be stamped by it with odious peculiarities. The man must be a prodigy who can retain his manners and morals undepraved by such circumstances." [2]

That Washington as a boy was "nursed, educated, and daily exercised in tyranny" is a fact. That he gradually overcame his inherited views on slavery is one of the things which entitle him to be classed as a great man.

Washington's formal education was rather short and at the age of sixteen we find him earning his living as a surveyor. Thomas Jefferson, speaking of Washington's education, said that it consisted of "merely reading, writing and common arithmetic to which he added surveying at a later day." He adds that Washington's mind was "slow in operation . . . being little aided by invention or imagination." [3]

In 1752, when his half-brother died, young Washington purchased his sister-in-law's share in the Mount Vernon estate, but owing to his military activities, it was not until 1759 that he was in a position to settle there and take charge of it. During this time (1752-59) he was engaged in the French and Indian war in which he won the reputation of being Virginia's foremost soldier and was put in charge of the militia of that colony. The ledgers and account books which he kept during this time show that he bought slaves whenever it was possible to replenish the eighteen slaves who were then working at Mount Vernon. In the account books of Washington, which are now kept in the Library of Congress at Washington, the entries show that in 1754 he bought two males and a female; in 1756, two males, two females and a child. Two years later he bought another male and in 1759, the year in which he was married, he bought thirteen slaves; in 1762, ten more; in 1764 seven more and in 1768 four. [4]

His wife, Martha, brought him thirty-nine "dower-Negroes." He kept a separate record of these Negroes all his life and mentions them as a separate unit in his will.

As a boy, Washington had made a trip to the West

Indies with his half-brother in which he had noted the poor conditions of the plantations there. This made him realize that only healthy, strong slaves were able to do a good day's work. Thus we find him giving much care to the health and proper management of his slaves. In respect to their mental and moral care we find him lacking. We know now that promiscuous sexual intercourse was allowed and that no one worried about their education or tried to alter these conditions, in the least.[5] In ignoring all concern for the moral and mental development of his slaves we find Washington in line with other gentlemen of eighteenth century Virginia who were obeying the law and furthering it according to the traditions in which they had been reared.

That Washington was not at all lax in the matter of looking after the health and management of his slaves, is easily proven. His diaries are full of entries like the following: — "January 28th, 1760, — found the new Negro Cupid ill of pleurisy at Dogue Run Quarter and had him brot home in a cart for better care of him." Again on February 2, of the same year,—"Breecky laid up this Morning with pains in his breast and head attended with fever."[6]

His diaries also prove Washington to have been a stern taskmaster. This was due, perhaps, to his training as a soldier and the love of precision and order which is part of the equipment of the successful surveyor. The entry for February 6th, 1760, reads as follows: "Passing by my Carpenters that were hughing, I found four of them, viz.: George, Tom, Mike and young Billy had only hughed 120 Foot yesterday from 10 O'Clock. Sat down therefore and observed. Tom and Mike in less space than 30 Minutes cleared the Bushes from abt. a poplar, stocklind it 10 Foot long and hughed each side 12 inches deep. Then, letting them proceed in their own way, they spent 25 minutes more in getting the cross cut saw standing to consider what to do, sawing the stock in two places, putting it on the Blocks, for hughing it, square lining it, ecta., and from this time till they had finished the stock entirely required 30 Minutes more; so that in the space of one hour and a quarter they each of them from the stump finished 20 Feet of hughing, from then it appears very clear, that allowing they work only from sun to sun and require two hours for Breakfast, they ought to yield each his 125 feet while the days are at their present length and more in proportion as they Increase. . . . While this was doing, George and Billy sawed 30 Foot of Plank, so that it appears as clear, making the same allowances as before (but not for the time required in piling the stock, etca.) they ought to saw 180 Feet of Plank. . . . It is to be observed here, that this hughing and sawing was of Poplar, what may be the difference therefore between the working of this Wood and other, some future observations must be known."[7]

This gives us some idea of Washington as an exacting manager. He demanded the full amount of work from his slaves but cannot be accused of being a harsh taskmaster. His treatment of his slaves was not unkind or brutal. When in 1762 he employed an overseer for all his slaves, the contract with the man specifies that he shall "take all necessary and proper care of the Negroes . . . using them with proper humanity and discretion."[8] Later on he told one of his managers to be "particularly attentive to my Negroes in their sickness." He makes the observation that overseers are apt "to view the poor creatures in scarcely any other light than they do a draft horse or ox, neglecting them as much when they are unable to work instead of comforting and nursing them when they lie on a sick bed." [9]

He believed that slave labor was cheaper than free labor, for we find him hiring a joiner in September, 1759, for a year's time. The joiner shall "use his best endeavors to instruct in the art of this trade any Negro or Negroes which George Washington shall cause to work with him during the twelfth month." [10]

When his slaves gave him trouble, they were shipped off to the West Indies. "Negro Tom" suffered this fate.[11]

Thus we can see that Washington was an exacting master, but not a cruel one. His training as a soldier made him demand the utmost discipline among them. The traditions in which he was brought up, confirmed the view that slavery was the best condition in which the Negro could live, and that Negro labor was not only a right but a necessity to the proper running of a plantation.

In 1759, long before the revolution seemed a possibility, we find Washington settled happily on his estate, a member of the House of Burgesses[12]; the most famous soldier in his colony; living the life of a country gentleman among his slaves and expecting to do so until the end of his days. In the same year he wrote, "I am now, I believe, fixed at this seat with an agreeable consort for life, and hope to find more happiness in retirement than I ever experienced amidst a wide and bustling world." [13]

## III.

### Washington's Pre-Revolutionary Views on Slavery

During the sixteen years which followed, between Washington's marriage and the outbreak of the revolution, we find him still replenishing his stock of slaves without the slightest feeling that there was anything immoral in doing so. An entry in his diary on July 25, 1768 reads: "Went to Alexandria and bought a Bricklayer from Mr. Piper and returned to dinner." [1] On June 11, 1770 he "went over to Colo. Thos. Moore's Sale and purchased two Negroes, to wit: Frank and James." [2] We know that in this year Washington paid taxes on eighty-seven slaves. [3]

Less than two weeks later, Washington signed a resolution framed by the "Association for the Counteraction of Various Acts of Oppression on the Part of Great Britain." This resolution read in part, "we will not import or bring into the Colony, or cause to be imported or brought into the Colony either by sea or land, any slaves, or make sale of any upon commission, or purchase any slave or slaves that may be imported by others, after the 1st day of November next, unless the same have been twelve months upon this continent." [4]

It is important to note that this resolution neither condemns slaveholding or the slave trade. It appears to have been drafted in a spirit of retaliation and is not in the least inspired by a moral disapproval of slavery.

We must not forget that during the period under consideration in this chapter, namely from 1759 to 1775, all the forces were at work which brought on the American Revolution. There is no place in this paper for a systematic statement of these causes. Most of them are stated in the Declaration of Independence. "The Stamp Tax" of 1765 increased the taxes of the colonists, and in the same year we find Washington complaining against "this unconstitutional method of taxation."[5]

On April 1, 1772, the House of Burgesses drafted a petition to the throne. Washington was a member of the House at this time. The petition reads in part: "the importation of slaves into the colonies from the coast of Africa hath long been considered as a trade of great inhumanity, and under its present encouragement we have too much reason to fear will endanger the very existence of your Majesty's American dominions."[6]

It is not to be forgotten that the Virginians at this time had nearly enough slaves for their plantations so that in reality they were not giving up so much as it might at first appear. It is of interest to note that the above petition is a complaint against slave importations from Africa which it calls "a trade of great inhumanity." That Washington was not so much impressed by the "inhumanity" of the case is clear; for he bought five more slaves in the same year.[7]

During the year before the outbreak of the Revolution, it was the custom for the people to meet in their town halls and court houses and air their views on the trend of affairs. In one of these meetings held at the court house of Fairfax County in Virginia, July 18, 1774, twenty-four resolutions were adopted by a committee of which Washington was chairman.

These Resolutions were known as "The Fairfax Resolves." One of them reads as follows:

"17. *Resolved*, that it is the opinion of this meeting, that, during our present difficulties and distress, no slaves ought to be imported into any of the British colonies on this continent; and we take this oppor-

tunity of declaring our most earnest wishes to see an
entire stop for ever put to such a wicked, cruel and
unnatural trade. . . ."

Inasmuch as Washington was the chairman of this
meeting, it seems hard to believe that these resolutions
were not representative of his own views, formed
after a study of the problem.

Jarred Sparks, a famous student of Washington and
a collector and publisher of his writings, says of the
above resolutions: "Such were the opinions of Washington, and his associates in Virginia, at the beginning
of the Revolutionary contest. The seventeenth resolve
merits attention, for the pointed manner in which
it condemns the slave-trade." [8]

We must not be led astray into thinking that a
condemnation of the "slave trade" was the same thing
as a condemnation of "the system" itself. It seems
inconsistent to condemn the "inhumanity" of the
trade and remain silent as to the "inhumanity" of the
system. But such are the facts.

It is a mistake to think that Virginia first complained about the importation of slaves so late as
Washington's day. In 1699 a tax of twenty shillings
was put upon each slave imported into the colony.[9]
Negroes increased so rapidly as to frighten the colonists so that Governor Spotswood in 1710 took measures to discourage their importation.[10] Again in 1732,
a duty of five percent was put on imported slaves to
last for a period of four years. This was revived and
extended. In 1740 another five percent was added,
and in 1754 five percent more was added. In 1759
a duty of twenty percent was put on all slaves brought
into Virginia from other American colonies.[11] It can
be seen then, that the need of slaves in Virginia was
not very great; on the contrary their number (over

100,000 in 1756) was large enough to be a cause of alarm. Raising slaves was thought cheaper than importing them.

All this explains, in a way, why Virginia could at the same time condemn the importation of slaves and approve the system of slavery. That is why the "Fairfax Resolves" cannot be taken as an index of the beliefs of those who signed them. The real reasons appear to have been threefold:

1. Virginia didn't need more slaves.
2. Prohibiting the importation of slaves was a retaliatory measure against Great Britain.
3. There were a few men who thought that slavery was inhuman.

George Washington appears not to have been one of these.[12] At the time that he assumed the command of the army at Cambridge, Mass., on July 3, 1775, there seems to be no evidence that he was not convinced of the righteousness and necessity of the slave system.

## IV.

### Washington's Attitude Toward Negroes As Soldiers

When Washington took command of the army in the summer of 1775, besides holding the view that the slave system was right and necessary, he held also the typical Southerner's prejudice against using Negroes as soldiers.

Before he reached Cambridge to assume command, he heard that the battle of Bunker Hill had been fought. It was a Negro, Peter Salem, who in this battle shot Major Pitcairn of the British forces, "as he mounted the redoubt shouting 'The Day is Ours!'" He is described as a "Negro soldier, once a slave"; also as a "colored patriot."[1]

Another Negro soldier named Salem Poor is mentioned in a petition to the General Court of Massachusetts Bay in which it is stated that he "behaved like an experienced officer, as well as an excellent soldier . . . in the person of this said Negro centres a brave and gallant soldier. The reward due to so great and distinguished a character, we submit to the Congress."

Did Washington know about these Negro heroes?

On May 20, 1775, the Committee of Safety of Massachusetts resolved that no slaves should be allowed to enlist. The resolution reads in part:

". . . that the admission of any persons as soldiers into the Army now raising, but only such as are Freemen, will be inconsistent with the principles that are to be supported, and reflect dishonor on this Colony: and that no Slaves be admitted into this Army upon any consideration whatever."[2]

In spite of this the historian, Bancroft, in his "History of the United States," tells us that

"the right of free Negroes to bear arms . . . was . . . as little disputed in New England as their other rights. They took their place . . . in the ranks with the white man, and their names may be read on the pension rolls of the country, side by side with those of other soldiers of the Revolution."[3]

The Connecticut and Rhode Island contingents contained Negro soldiers. In the former state, "some hundreds of blacks—slaves and freemen—were enlisted"; in the latter, "the names of colored men were entered with those of white citizens on the rolls of the militia." [4] We can see then that it was a decidedly mixed army; an army composed of white and black soldiers that Washington took command of, and it can be imagined how distasteful it was for him and how contrary to his traditional views.

General Gates, Washington's Adjutant General, began the movement to exclude Negroes from the army by issuing the following orders to the officers in charge of the recruiting: "You are not to enlist any . . . deserter from the ministerial army, nor any stroller, Negro, or vagabond. . . ." [5] As we have seen, Massachusetts had already prohibited the enlisting of slaves, so that these orders referred only to free Negroes.

About this time, Lord Dunmore, the Colonial Governor of Virginia, issued a proclamation, dated November 7, 1775, in which he said: "I do hereby further declare all indentured servants, Negroes, or others, free, that are able and willing to bear arms. . . ." [6]

In thinking over the possibilities of this British proclamation, Washington saw at once how dangerous it was. The old fear of the planter of the slave uprising made him act in haste. He wrote his secretary, Reed, on December 15, 1775, that "If Virginians are wise, that arch-traitor to the rights of humanity, Lord Dunmore, should be instantly crushed . . . otherwise like a snow-ball, in rolling, his army will get size, some through promises and some through inclination, joining his standard; but that which renders the measure indispensably necessary, is the Negroes. . . ." [7] To his friend, Richard Henry Lee, he wrote eleven days later: ". . . his strength will increase like a snow-ball, by rolling; and faster, if some expedient cannot be hit upon to convince slaves and servants of the impotency of his design." [8]

There seems to be no doubt that Washington was

alarmed about the situation, for we find him writing to the President of the Congress on December 31, 1775:

"It has been presented to me, that the free Negroes, who have served in this army, are very much dissatisfied at being discarded. As it is to be apprehended, that they may seek employ in the ministerial (British) army, I have presumed to depart from the resolution respecting them, and have given license for their being enlisted. If this is disapproved by Congress, I will put a stop to it." [9]

In the above we find Washington willing to put up with Negroes in his army because he fears they may seek to enlist "in the ministerial army." Washington had changed his policy regarding Negroes as soldiers. His alarm was so great that he acted even before the approval of Congress.

On January 16, 1776, a Committee in Congress decided "that the free Negroes who have served faithfully in the army at Cambridge may be re-enlisted therein, but no others." [10]

There is plenty of proof that many Negroes who had not been previously enlisted were taken into the army. From the diary of a Hessian officer, we learn that "no regiment is to be seen in which there are not Negroes in abundance; and among them there are able-bodied, strong and brave fellows." [11]

Thus we find Washington, the Virginian slaveholder, who at first disapproved of Negroes serving as soldiers in the army, actually in command of them. He, who had regarded the Negro as little better than a beast, was now urging them on to perform deeds of bravery on the battlefield along with their white brothers.

## V.

### Washington and Phillis Wheatley, Slave Poetess

As Washington's policy regarding the enlistment of
Negro soldiers was changing, something occurred
which was against his whole training and beliefs as a
Southern gentleman and slaveholder. Toward the
end of October, 1775, he received the following poem
in his mail:

"Celestial choir! enthron'd in realms of light
Columbia's scenes of glorious toils I write.
While freedom's cause her anxious breast alarms,
She flashes dreadful in refulgent arms.
See mother earth her offspring's fate bemoan,
And nations gaze at scenes before unknown!
See the bright beams of heaven's revolving light
Involved in sorrows and the veil of night!
The goddess comes, she moves divinely fair
Olive and laurel binds her golden hair:
Wherever shines this nature of the skies,
Unnumber'd charms and recent graces rise.
Muse! bow propitious while my pen relates
How pour her armies through a thousand gates;
As when Eolus heaven's fair face deforms,
Enrapped in tempest and a night of storms;
Astonished ocean feels the wild uproar,
The refluent surges beat the sounding shore,
Or thick as leaves in Autumn's golden reign,
Such, and so many, moves the warrior's train.
In bright array they seek the work of war,
Where high unfurl'd the ensign waves in air.
Shall I to Washington their praise recite?
Enough thou know'st them in fields of fight,
Thee, first in place and honours,—we demand

The grave and glory of thy martial bond.
Fam'd for thy valour, for thy virtues more,
Here every tongue thy guardian aid implore!
One century scarce performed its destined round,
When Gallic powers Columbia's fury found.
And so may you, whoever dares disgrace
The land of freedom's heaven-defended race!
Fix'd are the eyes of nations on the scales,
For in their hopes Columbia's arm prevails.
Anon Britannia droops the pensive head,
While round increase the rising hills of dead.
Oh! cruel blindness to Columbia's state!
Lament thy thirst of boundless powers too late.
Proceed great chief, with virtue on thy side,
Thy every action let the goddess guide.
A crown, a mansion, and a throne that shine,
With gold unfading, Washington be thine." [1]

With this poem was enclosed the following letter:

"Providence,
"October 26, 1775

"Sir,

"I have taken the freedom to address your Excellency in the enclosed poem, and entreat your acceptance though I am not insensible of its inaccuracies. Your being appointed by the Grand Continental Congress to be Generalissimo of the Armies of North America, together with the fame of your virtues, excite sensations not easy to suppress. Your generosity, therefore, I presume, will pardon the attempt. Wishing your Excellency all possible success in the great cause you are engaged in, I am

"Your Excellency's most obedient and humble servant,         "PHILLIS WHEATLEY" [2]

Washington, as one can imagine, was very busy planning his campaign when this poem and letter arrived. Accordingly he set it to one side, and it is not until February 10, 1776, that he sent the poem to Reed, his secretary in Philadelphia, with the following comment, "I recollect nothing else worth giving you the trouble of unless you can be amused by reading a letter and poem addressed to me by a Miss Phillis Wheatley." [3]

The following is Washington's reply dated Cambridge, February 28, 1776:

"MISS PHILLIS:—Your favor of the 26th of October did not reach my hands till the middle of December. Time enough, you will say, to have given an answer ere this. Granted. But a variety of important occurrences, continually interposing to distract the mind and withdraw the attention, I hope will apologize for the delay, and plead my excuse for the seeming, but not real neglect. I thank you most sincerely for your polite notice of me in the elegant lines you enclosed; and however undeserving I may be of such encomium and panegyric, the style and manner exhibit a striking proof of your poetical talents; in honor of which, and as a tribute justly due you, I would have published the poem, had I not been apprehensive that, while I only meant to give the world this new instance of your genius, I might have incurred the imputation of vanity. This, and nothing else, determined me not to give it a place in the public prints.

"If you ever come to Cambridge, or near headquarters, I shall be happy to see a person favored by the Muses, and to whom nature has been so liberal and beneficient in her dispensations. I am, with great respect, your obedient, humble servant." [4]

According to both Ford and Sparks, this letter is addressed to "Miss Phillis." Phillis Wheatley was not married at the time but later became a Mrs. Peters. Upon her death, her husband claimed all her papers, so that the original of this letter has never been found.[5] In the Congressional Library, copies of all of Washington's correspondence are on file and here the letter as copied is addressed to "Mrs. Phillis Wheatley." It is a question as to whether the letter was correctly copied. What we want to know is whether Washington knew that he was addressing a slave in the above letter.

This all seems rather trivial, but on the other hand it is most important for many writers have quoted this letter as proof of Washington's kind-hearted and democratic spirit towards a slave Negress.

It seems fairly clear to the writer that Washington knew that Phillis Wheatley was a Negress, for in the above letter he says "I would have published the poem . . . . to give the world this new instance of your genius." This all seems to point to the fact that Washington knew that she had written other poems and had perhaps even heard that she had published a volume of poems in London in 1773.

Again the fact that he used only "Miss" or "Mrs." shows that he was presumably acquainted with her race, for it was not the custom to address white ladies without using their surname. The letter should have been addressed "Mrs. Wheatley" or "Miss Wheatley." Thus we are rather forced to assume that Washington knew he was addressing a slave Negress when he answered her letter. That he consented to address her as "Miss" or "Mrs." is a tremendous advance beyond the ethics of a Virginia slaveholder, and that he asked her to visit him at his Cambridge headquarters, shows us an entirely new Washington—a broader and more human character.

Lossing[6] tells us that she accepted the invitation and that "she passed half an hour with the Commander-in-Chief, from whom and his officers, she received marked attention."

## VI.

### The Effect of the War on Washington's Views Towards "Free Negroes" As Soldiers

In July 1776, after the fighting had been going on for about a year, all hope of reconciliation was given up. And the Declaration of Independence was drawn up. This Declaration of Independence, in which the colonies declared their freedom from the British crown, had been largely intrusted to Jefferson, although the aged Franklin, John Adams, Roger Sherman, and Robert Livingston were members of the committee. Jefferson presented his first crude draft of the document to these men, who were on the whole so pleased with it that with very few changes it was approved. One of the changes not approved later by Congress was the following:—

"He (George III) has waged cruel war against human nature itself, violating its most sacred rights of life and liberty in the persons of a distant people who never offended him, captivating and carrying them into slavery in another hemisphere, or to incur miserable death in their transportation thither. This piratical warfare, the opprobrium of infidel powers, is the warfare of the Christian king of Great Britain. Determined to open a market where men should be bought and sold, he has prostituted his negative for suppressing every legislative attempt to prohibit or to restrain this execrable commerce. And that this assemblage of horrors might want no fact of distinguished die, he is now exciting those very people to rise in arms among us and to purchase that liberty of which he has deprived them, by murdering the people on whom he also obtruded them: thus paying off former crimes committed against the liberties of one people, with crimes which he urges them to commit against the lives of another." [1]

In his Autobiography, a document written shortly before his death, Jefferson, referring to this clause of the Declaration, says:

"The clause too, reprobating the enslaving the inhabitants of Africa, was struck out in complaisance to South Carolina and Georgia, who had never attempted to restrain the importation of slaves, and who, on the contrary, wished to continue it. Our Northern brethren also, I believe, felt a little tender under those censures; for though their people had very few slaves themselves, yet they had been pretty considerable carriers of them to others." [2]

We can see by Jefferson's explanation that the far South, South Carolina and Georgia, did not share the views of Virginia regarding the slave trade. The reason was that they needed more slaves to work the newly settled land whereas Virginia had slaves enough. Rather than cause a split between the colonies at this critical time, Jefferson and the Virginians overlooked it. This was a victory of politics over principles.

The following winter, that of 1776, was the most discouraging time in the whole war for Washington. Thousands of his soldiers died of hardship and exposure while intrigues were carried out in Congress to dispose of him as Commander-in-Chief and put some one else in his place. During that terrible winter at Valley Forge Washington estimated that he must find new recruits for his army before the spring campaigns should begin. In this desperate situation he must have been tempted to enlist Negroes. However, his Southern traditions held him back.

On January 2, 1778, General Varnum of Rhode Island, wrote to Washington saying, "A battalion of Negroes can be easily raised here." [3] On the same day Washington wrote as follows to the Governor of Rhode Island, "Inclosed you will receive a copy of a letter from General Varnum to me, upon the means which might be adopted for completing the Rhode Island troops to their full proportion in the Continental Army. I have nothing to say, in addition to what I wrote on the 29th of last month on this important subject." [4]

Surely this is a new Washington and not the same man who objected to enlisting Negroes in the army three years before. Now he "has nothing to say" about raising a battalion of Negroes.

On January 28, 1778, we find Washington writing to a Committee of the Congress, "The difficulty of getting waggoners and the enormous wages given them would tempt one to try any expedient to answer the end on easier and cheaper terms.

"Among others, it has occurred to me, whether it would not be eligible to hire Negroes in Carolina, Virginia and Maryland for the purpose. They ought, however, to be freemen for slaves could not be sufficiently depended on. It is to be apprehended that they would too frequently desert to the enemy to obtain their liberty, and for the profit of it, or to conciliate a more favorable reception would carry off their waggon horses with them." [5]

Surely we have a changed Washington here. A Washington commanding Negroes in the line, and who has "nothing to say" about a battalion of them which was being raised in Rhode Island; going so far as to recommend their use in the South where the majority of white men were strongly prejudiced against them! It is important to note, however, that up to this time only free Negroes had with approval been used. But what did Washington think about using slaves as soldiers?

## VII.

### Washington's and Hamilton's Views on Negro Slaves As Soldiers

In the first few months of 1778, while Washington's correspondence with General Varnum and Governor Cooke of Rhode Island was in progress, one of his aide-de-camps, a Lieutenant Colonel John Laurens of South Carolina, wrote a letter to his father from headquarters proposing a plan to increase the manpower of his state "from an untried source." In South Carolina the British forces were enlisting slaves who ran away from their masters and there were so few white men in proportion to the Negroes that most of them had to stay on their plantations to guard their property. This was a dangerous situation because it looked as if South Carolina would not be able to raise its quota of troops for the next campaign. To remedy this situation, young Col. Laurens wrote the following letter to his father:

"I would advance those who are unjustly deprived of the rights of mankind (the slaves) to a state which would be a proper gradation between abject slavery and perfect liberty, and besides I am persuaded that if I could obtain authority for the purpose, I would have a corps of such men trained, uniformly clad, equipped and ready in every respect to act at the opening of the next campaign. The ridicule that may be thrown on the color I despise, because I am sure of rendering essential service to my country."

It seems remarkable that the son of a South Carolina slaveholder should speak of slaves "being unjustly deprived of the rights of mankind." There can be no doubt that Col. Laurens got his ideas from his father, Henry Laurens, who on August 14, 1776 had written to his son:

"I abhor slavery. . . . I found the Christian religion and slavery growing under the same authority. . . . I nevertheless disliked it. Not less than twenty thousand pounds sterling would all my Negroes produce if sold at public auction tomorrow. I am not the man who enslaved them; they are indebted to Englishmen for that favor; nevertheless I am devising means for manumitting many of them. Great powers oppose me—the laws and customs of my country. What will my children say if I deprive them of so much estate?" [1]

Col. Laurens wrote again to his father from Washington's headquarters on February 2, 1778:

"You ask, what is the General's (Washington's) opinion upon this subject? He is convinced that the various tribes of blacks in the southern parts of the continent, offer a resource to us that should not be neglected. With respect to my particular plan he only objects to it, with the argument of pity for a man who should be less rich than he might." [2]

Thus we see that Washington regards the slaves as a "resource" to the South and although he was not prepared to recommend Col. Laurens' scheme, he was against the idea of freeing the Laurens slaves because of the loss in money to their owner.

Now, young Col. Laurens had a friend at headquarters, no other than Alexander Hamilton, who later became America's first and greatest Secretary of the Treasury. Hamilton was only twenty years old at the time and a friendship developed between him and Col. Laurens. It is known that Hamilton was in sympathy with his friend's scheme to enlist Negroes in the army. When Col. Laurens went South for that purpose he had with him a letter of Hamilton's addressed to the President of Congress which read in part:

"Col. Laurens, who will have the honor of delivering you this letter, is on his way to South Carolina, on a project . . . to raise two, three or four battalions of Negroes . . . he will give you a detail of his plan, he wishes to have recommended by Congress to the state. . . .

"It appears to me, that an expedient of this kind, in the present state of Southern affairs, is the most rational that can be adopted. . . . Indeed I can hardly see how a sufficient force can be collected in that quarter without it. . . . I have not the least doubt, that the Negroes will make very excellent soldiers, with proper management, and I will venture to pronounce, that they cannot be put in better hands than those of Mr. Laurens. He has all the zeal, intelligence, enterprise, etc., etc. . . . requisite to succeed. It is a maxim with some great military judges, that, with sensible officers, soldiers can hardly be too stupid; and, on this principle, it is thought that the Russians would make the best troops in the world, if they were under other officers than their own. The King of Prussia (Frederic the Great) is among the number who maintain this doctrine; and has a very emphatic saying on the occasion, which I do not exactly recollect. I mention this because I hear it frequently objected to the scheme of embodying Negroes, that they are too stupid to make soldiers. This is so far from appearing to me a valid objection, that I think their want of cultivation (for their natural faculties are as good as ours). . . . Let officers be men of sense and sentiment; and the nearer the soldiers approach to machines, perhaps the better.

"I foresee that this project will have to combat much opposition from prejudice and self-interest. The contempt we have been taught to entertain for the blacks, makes us fancy many things that are founded neither in reason nor experience; and an unwillingness to part with property of so valuable a kind, will furnish a thousand arguments to show the impracticability, or pernicious tendency, of a scheme which requires such sacrifices. But it should be considered, that if we do not make use of them in this way, the enemy probably will: and that the best way to counteract the temptations they will hold out, will be to offer them ourselves. An essential part of the plan is to give them their freedom with their swords. This will secure their fidelity, animate their courage, and, I believe, will have a good influence upon those that remain, by opening a door to their emancipation. This circumstance, I confess, has no small weight in inducing me to wish the success of the project; for the dictates of humanity and true policy, equally interest me in favor of this unfortunate class of men. . . ." [3]

We can see from the above letter that Hamilton was in sympathy with the plan of his friend, Col. Laurens. Hamilton was aware that it would have "to combat much opposition from prejudice and self-interest"; however, he thought the plan a "very good one."

On March 16, 1779, just a few days after Hamilton wrote the above letter, Col. Laurens' father wrote Washington:

". . . the country is distressed and will be more so, unless further reenforcements are sent to its relief. Had we arms for three thousand such black men as I could select in Carolina, I should have no doubt of success in driving the British out of Georgia, and subduing east Florida before the end of July." [4]

Washington's reply to this letter, dated March 20, 1779, said in part:

". . . The policy of our arming slaves is in my opinion a moot point, unless the enemy set the example. For, should we begin to form battalions of them, I have not the smallest doubt, if the war be prosecuted, of their following us in it, and justifying the measure upon our own ground. The contest then must be, who can arm fastest. And where are our arms? Besides I am not clear that a discrimination will not render slavery more irksome to those who remain in it. Most of the good and evil things in this life are judged of by comparison; and I fear a comparison in this case will be productive of much discontent in those, who are held in servitude. But as this is a subject that has never employed much of my thoughts, these are no more than the first crude ideas that have struck me upon the occasion." [5]

It is curious to note that a year before the letter was written, Washington knew that slaves were being used in the Negro battalions that were raised in Rhode Island. Washington had had "nothing to say" in his reply to the governor, but that doesn't mean that he was not aware that slaves had been enlisted in Rhode Island. The Bill which the Rhode Island legislature passed read, "Whereas . . . Gen. Washington hath inclosed to this state a proposal made to him by Brigadier-General Varnum, to enlist . . . such slaves as should be willing," etc. [6] This seems to prove conclusively that Washington knew that slaves had been enlisted in Rhode Island the previous year. Why, then, was the enlisting of slaves in South Carolina, "a moot point"? The only probably answer to this question is that Washington knew that the people in South Carolina would never sanction this scheme of Col. Laurens. He didn't want to irritate these Southerners unnecessarily. In more than one place in Washington's life we find the politician running away with his principles.

In refraining from recommending that South Carolina enlist Negro slaves as soldiers, Washington showed keen political insight. On March 29, 1779 a committee in Congress did finally approve Col. Laurens' "scheme." The people of South Carolina were very angry about the resolutions and even proposed remaining neutral until the end of the war.

Meanwhile, Col. Laurens kept up his fight in South Carolina for the raising of the Negro slave battalions. When in August of 1781 the report of the Special

Committee on Raising the Negro Soldiers in these two states seemed to be definitely held up, Col. Laurens wrote to his friend Alexander Hamilton: "I had, in fact, resumed the black project . . . . but I was out-voted, having only reason on my side, and being opposed by a triple-headed monster, that shed the baneful influence of avarice, prejudice and pusillanimity, in all our assemblies." [7] Referring to conditions in Georgia, he wrote to Washington on May 19, 1782: "We shall be out voted there . . . as we have been in this country" [8] (South Carolina).

Washington answered this letter of Col. Laurens in July, 1782. He said in part, "I must confess that I am not at all astonished at the failure of your plan. That spirit of freedom which at the commencement of this contest would have gladly sacrificed everything to the attainment of its object, has long since subsided, and every selfish passion has taken its place. It is not the public, but the private interest, which influences the generality of mankind, nor can the Americans any longer boast an exception. Under these circumstances, it would rather have been surprising if you had succeeded, nor will you, I fear, have better success in Georgia." [9]

Here we find Washington deploring the lack of the "spirit of freedom which . . . would have gladly sacrificed"—even to the extent of allowing Negro slaves to be enlisted as an emergency. This raises the question as to whether he had changed his opinion as to the enlisting of Negro slaves in the South. Was it still a "moot point" with him or not? Did he perhaps think it unnecessary to repeat again the sentiments he had expressed when writing to the Colonel's father two years earlier? There can be no definite answer to these questions. In any case we find a Washington with a much higher opinion of the Negro as a fighter and as a man. A Washington who had learned by experience that a slave is also a human being and should be treated as such.

## VIII.

### Washington's Reaction to Lafayette's Proposals

On October 19, 1781, the British commander, Lord Cornwallis, surrendered at Yorktown and General Lafayette, who had done so much to help America win her independence, returned to France in December of that year. About two years later on February 5, 1783, Lafayette wrote the following to Washington:

"Now, my dear General, that you are going to enjoy some ease and quiet, permit me to propose a plan to you, which might become greatly beneficial to the black part of mankind. Let us unite in purchasing a small estate, where we may try the experiment to free the Negroes, and use them only as tenants. Such an example as yours might render it a general practice; and if we succeed in America, I will cheerfully devote a part of my time to render the method fashionable in the West Indies. If it be a wild scheme, I had rather be mad in this way, than to be thought wise in the other task." [1]

Washington replied to this letter on April 5, 1783, in part as follows:

"The scheme, my dear Marquis, which you propose as a precedent to encourage the emancipation of the black people in this country from the state of bondage in which they are held, is a striking evidence of the benevolence of your heart. I shall be happy to join you in so laudable a work, but will defer going into a detail of the business till I have the pleasure of seeing you." [2]

It should not be forgotten that Washington was still in the army when he received the above letter from Lafayette and still in military service when his reply was written. Wars do not end on the day peace is declared, and there was much to be done before the land could return once more to the status of peace. Among the problems which arose at this time was that of the disposition of slaves who had enlisted in the army. These slaves were classed in four general groups:

1. Slaves who had run away from their masters to enlist.

2. Slaves who had been sent to serve in the place of their masters.

3. Slaves who had been purchased by the government from their masters for soldiers.

4. Slaves who had enlisted with the promise of being freed at the end of the war.

When the war ended there was a rush of masters who claimed their slaves as property in spite of the fact that these same Negroes had endangered their lives for American liberty. Washington determined that these slaves who had served their country so faithfully should not be handed back indiscriminately to their masters. Accordingly, when the petitions of owners came to his attention he ordered "a court of inquiry, consisting of five as respectable officers as can be found . . . to examine the validity of the claim, the manner in which the person in question came into service, and the propriety of his being discharged or retained in service." A postcript added, "All concerned should be notified to attend." [3]

We have seen that a slave in the Virginia of Washington's boyhood had absolutely no rights against his master, but here we find Washington setting up a court of justice in which a Negro would have a right to fight the unjust claim of his master. Surely this is a changed Washington from the Virginia slave-holder of pre-revolutionary times!

In the treaty of peace which was signed by Great Britain at the end of the war, it was specifically stipulated therein that the British Armies should withdraw, "without carrying away any Negroes, or other property of the American inhabitants."[4]

Now, it is wrong to think that Washington had fallen into any sentimental love of Negroes. In fact, his mind was primarily legalistic and an objective survey of his life shows that he was far more concerned with problems of "right" than of principles. It is not surprising, then, to find him writing the following letter to Mr. Parker, an American who was appointed to see that the British carried out the letter of the law in their embarkation:

April 28, 1783

"Some of my own slaves (writes Washington), and those of Mr. Lund Washington who lives at my house, may probably be in New York, but I am unable to give you their description—their names being so easily changed, it will be fruitless to give you. If by chance, you should come at the knowledge of any of them, I will be much obliged by your securing them, so that I may obtain them again." [5]

This letter shows conclusively that Washington

was still in favor of slavery as a system, at least when it affected his own rights and pocket. This is the man who had condemned the people of South Carolina for their "private interest." This places Washington up until this time among "the generality of mankind," to employ his own words. We begin to see that Washington was a very human "plaster-saint" and that a good deal of moral casuistry lay behind those pious, dignified features.

Before leaving the army, Washington, on June 8, 1783, sent out a circular letter to all the Governors of the United States. This letter is important because it contains his views as to the future "well-being" of his country. Here he says, "There are four things, I humbly conceive, are essential to the well-being, I may venture to say, to the existence of the United States, as an independent power. First, An indissoluble union of the states under one federal head. Second, A Sacred regard to public justice. Third, The adoption of a proper peace establishment. Fourth, The prevalence of that pacific and friendly disposition among the people of the United States which will induce them to forget their local prejudices and policies; to make those mutual concessions, which are requisite to the general prosperity; and in some instances, to sacrifice their individual advantages to the interest of the community." [6]

Does it not seem strange that Washington remains silent as to the whole problem of slavery? The more so, when we recollect that not more than two months before he had written to Lafayette that he would be happy to join him "in so laudable a work" . . . "to encourage the emancipation of the black people in this country." Why was the whole subject of slavery ignored in the above circular letter?

The answer seems to be that Washington felt that unity was the most important thing at this time and that he was afraid of introducing a subject which was apt to cause divergence between the states. His silence was after all, perhaps the part of wisdom. Who at this early date could have possibly foreseen that slavery should be the rock upon which the union would nearly split? That Washington was one of the few of his countrymen who became conscious of this danger, I hope to show on a later page.

Washington gave up his commission in the army and retired to his Mount Vernon estate in December of 1783. Here he expected to spend the rest of his days "in the practise of domestic virtues." [7] In the summer of the following year, Lafayette visited him for a few days, continuing on to England. What did these two men decide about the experiment to free the Negroes and employ them only as tenants, which Lafayette had proposed in his letter? To this letter Washington had replied that he would put the matter off "until I have the pleasure of seeing you." The two men were now together and it would be interesting to know what Washington said to his friend. There are, however, no records on this point, as Washington, due to the stress of the war, had been forced to give up his habit of keeping a diary. It is hard to believe that the two men didn't discuss the project, even though there are no records of it, for it was a favorite hobby of the great Frenchman. To show how strongly he felt I quote a letter of Lafayette's to John Adams, who became president after Washington:

"In the case of my black brethren, I feel myself warmly interested, and most decidedly side, so far as respects them, against the white part of mankind. Whatever be the complexion of the enslaved, it does not, in my opinion, alter the complexion of the crime which the enslaver commits,—a crime much blacker than any African face. It is to me a matter of great anxiety and concern, to find that this trade is sometimes perpetrated under the flag of liberty, our dear and noble stripes, to which virtue and glory have been constant standard-bearers." [8]

It will be remembered that Lafayette had written Washington inviting him to enter into an experiment with him in which a small estate was to be purchased and free Negroes employed as tenants. We know that Lafayette had no idea of giving up his plan.

On May 10, 1786, nearly two years after Lafayette's visit, Washington wrote him the following letter from his Mount Vernon estate:

"The benevolence of your heart, my dear Marquis, is so conspicuous upon all occasions, that I never wonder at any fresh proofs of it; but your late purchase of an estate in the colony of Cayenne, with a view of emancipating the slaves on it, is a generous and noble proof of your humanity. Would to God a like spirit might diffuse itself generally into the minds of the people of this country! But I despair of seeing it. Some petitions were presented to the Assembly, at its last session, for the abolition of slavery; but they could scarcely obtain a reading. To set the slaves afloat at once would, I really believe, be productive of much inconvenience and mischief; but, by degrees it certainly might, and assuredly ought to be, effected, and that too, by legislative authority." [9]

It must be remembered that Lafayette had actually put his plan into effect near Cayenne in French

Guiana. What was it that held Washington back from joining his friend in this experiment and lending the weight of his reputation to the venture? Could it have been politics, or a desire not to offend the American slaveholders in the far South that held him back?

It is interesting to note how far Washington had gone beyond the traditions of his boyhood. He was now quite willing to admit that Negro slavery "by degrees certainly might" be abolished. He even went so far as to say that it "ought to be abolished." This meant that for Washington, the righteousness of the system was in grave question. He had even given the matter enough thought to suggest that the solution "ought to be effected . . . by legislative authority."

As for Lafayette's Cayenne experiment, it was shortly to be a failure, for the Marquis was soon thrown into prison and his Negroes sold by order of the National Convention. Even in prison he showed interest for the experiment and wrote the following to the Princess d'Hénin while imprisoned in Magdeburg March 15, 1793:

"I know not what disposition has been made of my plantation at Cayenne; but I hope Madame de Lafayette will take care that the Negroes, who cultivate it, shall preserve their liberty." [10]

## IX

### Wavering Principles, 1785-1787

In 1785 Washington was living the life of a country gentleman at Mount Vernon and had renewed his old custom of keeping a diary. The entry of May 26, 1785, reads:

"Upon my return found Mr. Magowan and a doctr. Coke and a Mr. Asbury here, the last two Methodist Preachers recommended by General Roberdeau." [1]

The Mr. Asbury referred to, was Francis Asbury, the first bishop of the Methodist Church in America. In the bishop's diary the following remark about the visit is entered:

"We waited on General Washington, who received us politely and gave us his opinion *against* slavery." [2]

Note that Washington's opinions were *against* slavery and not just *about* slavery. That this feeling against slavery hadn't altered the system at Mount Vernon is plain, for Washington was still dependent upon them for labor. On February 18, 1786, the total number of slaves on the estate was 216.[3] In April of the same year he wrote to Robert Morris regarding slavery, saying:

"I can only say, that there is not a man living, who wishes more sincerely than I do, to see a plan adopted for the abolition of it; but there is only one proper and effectual mode by which it can be accomplished, and that is by legislative authority; and this as far as my suffrage will go, shall never be wanting." [4]

In the fall of the same year he wrote the following letter to a Mr. John Fr. Mercer:

"I never mean—unless some particular circumstance should compel me to it—to possess another slave by purchase; it being among my first wishes to see some plan adopted, by which slavery in this country may be abolished by slow, sure and imperceptible degrees." [5]

"Some particular circumstance" must take place

before Washington could be compelled to buy another slave. This appears to be putting the blame for slavery on the economic *necessity* of the system. Washington, as we have seen, began to doubt that slavery was a necessary system, however he was quite ready to commit himself and say that he would never buy another slave. The question is how big were the "circumstances" that stood between him and the purchase of another slave.

Two months later we find him writing again to Mr. Mercer:

"Although," he says, "I have great repugnance to increasing my slaves by purchase: yet as it seems so inconvenient for you to make payment by other modes, . . . I will take five more Negroes of you, if you can spare such as will answer my purpose upon the terms offered in your former letter," etc., etc.[6]

How can one make such a hair splitting distinction as Washington does here? Is there much difference between his taking the Negroes as a payment, or paying for them? Certainly not much difference!

Here is another letter written some three months later to Henry Lee. Washington says:

"It is not my wish to be your competitor in the purchase of any of M. Hunter's tradesmen; especially as *I am in a great degree principled against increasing my number of slaves by purchase.* . . . Yet if you are not disposed to buy the bricklayer which is advertised for sale, for your own use . . . and his price does not exceed one hundred, or a few more pounds, *I should be glad if you should buy him for me.* I have much work in this way to do this summer. If he has a family, with which he is to be sold; or from whom he would reluctantly part, I decline the purchase; his feelings I would not be the means of hurting in the latter case, nor at any rate be incumbered with the former." [7]

Here we still have Washington the buyer of his fellow men, despite his humane sentiments about not separating the poor bricklayer from his family if he happened to have one. We can now measure how great the particular circumstance would have to be to make him act against his principles. In this case the circumstance was that "I have much work in this way to do this summer." This was the particular circumstance which was to compel him to buy a bricklayer three months before the Continental Congress convened in Philadelphia. We find that Washington's principles were, in spite of his good intentions, subject to his economic needs. That Henry Lee "should buy him for me" is no excuse at all— nothing but a technicality.

## X.

### Washington at the Constitutional Convention, 1787

It will be my task to report on the debates in the Constitutional Convention only in so far as they refer to the problem of Negro slavery. As Washington was not only present, but for a time the presiding officer, it is important to know not only what happened, but what reaction these events had upon him.

The Convention met at Philadelphia toward the end of May, 1787, and Washington, who was a delegate from Virginia, was elected to preside over it. The purpose of the Convention was to frame a Constitution for the United States, so that some strong central form of government could be set up to displace the weak Confederation of States which appeared to be too weak to hold the country together and inspire confidence abroad. The debts which America owed to other countries were still unpaid although the war had been ended for four years. Selfish interests had sprung up in various states which threatened the unity of the nation. These were some of the most important reasons why the Convention was held.

The debates were held behind closed doors and some of them were very poorly recorded while others escaped into thin air. It was a time of great confusion and it appears that Washington, although relieved of his duties as presiding officer for over a period of two weeks and therefore in a position to take an active part in the debates, remained altogether silent when matters pertaining to slavery were discussed.

There is no place here to give an outline of all these discussions as it would lead us too far afield.[1] The problems discussed which had a bearing on slavery were:

1. Whether slaves were just "property" or human beings as well.

2. Should the slaves be counted the same as white people in the representation of the states in Congress? If not, in what proportion?

3. Should the importation of slaves stop at once, or if not, how long should it continue?

It is not hard to imagine the divergence in the views of the North and South on these points. It was a time when great concessions had to be made in order that the Union be preserved. The outcome was that slaves were to be considered still as property; that each five Negroes should count as one white franchise; and that the slave trade should be allowed to continue for another twenty years until 1808. These were the three great compromises made between the North and the South regarding slavery. It must not be thought that the South of these early times was the South as we know it today; for, it was only South Carolina and Georgia which insisted that the slave trade be continued.

It must have been purely in the interest of the Union that Washington remained silent. It was the Union which he held to be the most important of all the points of issue; this should be preserved even at the cost of humiliating concessions which seemed sure to appear later in the course of the young nation.

Washington was not entirely satisfied with the Constitution. He felt that it was a compromise and that the problem of slavery might come up again to disturb the Union. Concerning it he said:

"There are some things in the new form (the Constitution) I will readily acknowledge, which never did, and I am persuaded never will, obtain my cordial approbation; but I did then conceive, and do now most firmly believe, that in the aggregate it is the best constitution, that can be obtained at this epoch, and that this, or a dissolution, awaits our choice, and is the only alternative."[2]

He had come to the Convention with the idea that slavery "ought" to be done away with by some form of legislation. He was not quite ready to say that slavery "must" be done away with; he was not ready to fight against the system. A born conservative, he despised anything which appeared of a radical nature. The slave system although not quite morally justifiable, was still thought by him to be a necessary evil, so necessary that he might at any time be "compelled" to buy another slave.

## XI.

### The Status of the Negro during the Presidency of Washington

Washington began his office as the first President of the United States on March 4, 1789. He had every reason to believe that the question of Negro slavery would not disturb him during his administration, for had not the Constitution settled the question for twenty years to come? But such was not to be the case, for no sooner had the new President taken office than the Quakers sent a memorial to Congress requesting laws be passed which should end the slave-trade.[1] It can be imagined how disturbed Washington was to have this troublesome problem brought up at a time when it was supposed, at least, to have been settled by the Constitution. He was not so opposed to the abolition of slavery itself; it was, he thought, not the right time to bring up the problem. A memorial was sent to Congress on February 3, 1790, by the Pennsylvania Abolition Society of which Benjamin Franklin was president, and no doubt Franklin himself had a hand in the writing of it. It read in part:—

"That—an association was formed several years since—for promoting the abolition of slavery,—That mankind are all formed by the same Almighty Being—and equally designed for the enjoyment of happiness, the Christian religion teaches us to believe, and the political creed of Americans fully coincides with the position from a persuasion that equal liberty was originally the portion, and is still the birth-right, of all men;—they earnestly entreat—that you will be pleased to countenance the restoration of liberty to those unhappy men, who alone, in this land of freedom, are degraded to perpetual bondage, . . . that you will devise means for removing this inconsistency from the character of the American people; that you will promote mercy and justice towards this distressed race; and that you will step to the very verge of the power vested in you for discouraging every species of traffic in the persons of our fellow men.

"Philadelphia, February 3, 1790

BENJAMIN FRANKLIN, *President*"[2]

The matter after much heated debate was referred to a committee in spite of the fact that those in favor of slavery insisted that the matter was covered in the Constitution and that Congress had no right to interfere.[3]

Washington's diary for March 16, 1790, reads:

"I was visited . . . by one of the people called Quakers; active in pursuit of Measures laid before Congress for emancipating the slaves; after much general conversation, and an endeavor to remove the prejudices which he said had been entertained of the motives by which the attending deputation from their society was actuated, he used arguments to show the immorality—injustice—and impolicy of keeping these people in a state of slavery; with declarations, however, that he did not wish for more than a gradual abolition, or to see any infraction of the Constitution to effect it. To these I replied, that as it was a matter which might come before me for official decision I was not inclined to express my sentiments on the merits of the question before this should happen."[4]

For a week after this entry in his diary, Congress debated the question and finally it was decided that Congress had no right to interfere with slavery until 1808 as the Constitution had settled the matter for the time being. On March 27, 1790, Washington wrote to David Stuart in part:

"The memorial of the Quakers (and a very mala-propos one it was) has at length been put to sleep, and will scarcely awaken before the year 1808." [5]

It appears that many Virginians had heard Congress was about to free the slaves, the result being that many were sold for trifling sums in the general alarm.

A year later, in 1791, Washington was forced to appeal through diplomatic channels to the Court of Spain regarding the many slaves who escaped over the Georgia boundary into Florida, then a Spanish possession.

In the same year Washington's lawyer took some of the Mount Vernon slaves to Philadelphia where they claimed they could not be returned to Virginia be-cause of a Pennsylvania law. Washington instructed one Tobias Lear to bring the slaves back to Virginia in a manner that would deceive both the slaves and the public. [6] This desire on the part of the President to deceive the public, shows how much Washington's conscience was bothering him. He didn't wish to bring the fact that he was a slave-owner before his countrymen, yet he was unwilling to lose such valuable property as slaves.

Three years later, in 1794, Washington wrote again to Tobias Lear concerning the sale of some of his lands in the West. In this letter he says he earnestly wishes

"to liberate a certain species of property—which I

possess very repugnantly to my own feelings; but which imperious necessity compels, and until I can substitute some other expedient, by which expenses, not in my power to avoid (however well I may be disposed to do it) can be defrayed." [7]

In the same year he wrote to Alexander Spotswood,

"As you have put the question I shall in a few words, give my ideas about it. Were it not then, that I am principled against selling Negroes, as you would cattle at a market, I would not in twelve months from this date, be possessed of one as a slave. I shall be happily mistaken if they are not found to be a very troublesome species of property ere many years pass over our heads." [8]

Here we get a picture of the aged President wishing sincerely that by some legal means emancipation would come. He even saw with prophetic vision, the dangers which the future held regarding slavery. The inconsistency of what he thought was right, and the economic necessity of his continuing as a slave-holder was worrying him in no small degree.

In 1795, a year after he had written the above letter to Alexander Spotswood, Washington advertised for one of his slaves who had run away. We learn from Haworth that north of Virginia, the President didn't allow his name to appear in the advertisement. Washington was again ashamed to face public criticism; he was again ready to deceive the public. There was in fact no legal reason why he could not have advertised. Washington's conscience was hurting him. He was ashamed.

Before Washington retired from the Presidency he delivered his now famous "Farewell Address." Here we find him extolling the Union as he had done thirteen years before upon his retirement from the army. He mentions various things which may give trouble to the Union, such as speaking of the North and the South as distinct geographical regions, "whence," he warns, "designing men may endeavor to excite a *belief* that there is a real difference of local interests and views." [9] But not a word of warning as to slavery! He lost the opportunity to condemn slavery and lend the weight of his great reputation to the cause of freedom and emancipation. He felt the danger of bringing up the problem of freeing the slaves at this time. He was still more interested and felt that it was more important to preserve the Union in good will than to venture upon such dangerous ground.

On December 11, 1796, in a letter to a certain John Sinclair, Washington gives us an economic argument against slavery:

"The present prices of lands in Pennsylvania are higher than in Maryland and Virginia, although they are not of superior quality."

He tells us that one of the reasons for this is that,

"There are laws here (in Pennsylvania) for the gradual abolition of slavery which neither of the two states above mentioned have at present, but which nothing is more certain than that they must have, and at a period not remote." [10]

What seems at first sight to have been a serious omission in his "Farewell Address" was perhaps, after all, the wisest course.

## XII.

### The Negro Slave in Washington's Will

Once again we find Washington home at Mount Vernon, but now there is no doubt but that his conscience is worrying him regarding slaveholding. In a letter dated August, 1797, he wrote to his nephew, Laurence Washington:

"I wish from my soul that the legislature of this state, could see the policy of gradual abolition of slavery. It might prevent much future mischief." [1]

The "future mischief" was to come some sixty-three years later when the Civil War broke out.

Before his death he possessed so many slaves that they had become a heavy responsibility for him. He had more slaves than his estate could support and in fact they were driving him slowly into bankruptcy. The same month he wrote to another nephew, Robert Lewis:

"It is demonstratively clear, that on this estate I have more working Negroes by a full moiety, than can be employed to any advantage in the farming system, and I shall never turn Planter thereon. To sell the surplus I cannot, because I am principled against this kind of traffic in the human species. To hire them out is almost as bad, because they could not be disposed of in families to any advantage, and to disperse the families I have an aversion. What then is to be done? Something must or I shall be ruined; for all the money (in addition to what I raise by crops, and rents) that have been received for Lands, sold within the last four years to the amount of fifty thousand dollars, has scarcely been able to keep me afloat." [2]

Here we have a Washington who admits having principles against the slave system. What is more, these principles are driving him toward financial ruin. "What then is to be done?" he asks. An answer to this question was not necessary for on the 14th of December, 1799, Washington had died. At his death he owned one hundred and twenty-four slaves, another one hundred and fifty-three belonged to his wife (the Dower Negroes), and forty others were leased from a neighbor.[3]

But this was not Washington's last word on slavery. To find that, we must quote an item from his last will and testament. This is the second item of his will and followed upon the bequest to his wife, Martha.

"Item—Upon the decease of my wife, it is my will and desire that all slaves whom I hold in my own right shall receive their freedom. To emancipate them during her life, would, though earnestly wished by me, be attended with such insuperable difficulties, on account of their intermixture by marriage with the Dower Negroes, as to excite the most painful sensations, if not disagreeable consequences to the latter, while both descriptions are in the occupancy of the same proprietor; it not being in my power, under the tenure by which the Dower Negroes are held, to manumit them. And whereas, among those who will receive freedom according to this devise, there may be some, who, from old age or bodily infirmities, and others, who, on account of their infancy, will be unable to support themselves, it is my will and desire, that all who come under the first and second description shall be comfortably clothed and fed by my heirs while they live; and that such of the latter description as have no parents living, or, if living, are unable or unwilling to provide for them, shall be bound by the court until they shall arrive at the age of twenty-five years; and in cases where no record can be produced, whereby their ages can be ascertained, the judgment of the court, upon its own view of the subject, shall be adequate and final. The Negroes thus bound are (by their masters or mistresses) to be taught to read and write, and to be brought up to some useful occupation, agreeably to the laws of the Commonwealth of Virginia providing for the support of orphan and other poor children. And I do hereby expressly forbid the sale or transportation out of the said Commonwealth, of any slave I may die possessed of, under any pretence whatsoever. And I do, moreover, most pointedly and most solemnly enjoin it upon my executors hereafter named, or the survivors of them, to see that this clause respecting slaves, and every part thereof, be religiously fulfilled at the epoch it is directed to take place, without evasion, neglect, or delay, after the crops which may then be on the ground be harvested, particularly as it respects the aged and infirm; seeing that a regular and permanent fund be established for their support, as long as there are subjects requiring it; not trusting to the uncertain provision to be made by individuals. And to my mulatto man, William, calling himself William Lee, I give immediate freedom; or, if he should prefer it (on account of the accidents which have befallen him, and which have rendered him incapable of walking or of any active employment), to remain in the situation he now is, it shall be optional in him to do so; in either case, however, I allow him an annuity of thirty dollars, during his natural life, which shall be independent of the victuals and clothes he has been accustomed to receive, if he chooses the last alternative;

but in full with his freedom if he prefers the first. And this I give him as a testimony of my sense of his attachment to me, and for his faithful services during the Revolutionary War." [4]

Washington's will was drawn up by himself about a year before his death;—drawn up "by an act in conformity with his whole career." Through this career it had always been his wish to free the slaves which he held in his own right, but owing to the complications caused by their having intermarried with the Dower Negroes—i.e. those brought to him by his wife Martha Curtiss—he found that it was not legally possible to free his own slaves without "insuperable difficulties" during his life.

He was careful that those of his slaves who were to be set free and were too old, were cripples, or too young to earn their livings, should be provided for. Nor did he wish any of his slaves sent outside of the commonwealth of Virginia or separated too far from their families. Although born in a slave-holding community and educated in an environment in sympathy with the institution, Washington's sincerest wish was to see slavery abolished by law and the slaves themselves set free.

As we have seen, he did not favor any quick or rash method of abolition and there are hints in one of his letters, quoted above, to Lafayette, that he, at one time at least, favored the experiment of colonization which ended so disastrously in the century that was to follow. The fact is that Washington acted as wisely and humanely as possible in treating with a problem, the solution of which time alone could solve. That he sensed the danger of the institution on American soil, and the absurdity of its practice under a

Constitution which proclaimed that one of its purposes was to "secure the Blessing of Liberty to ourselves and our posterity," is evident. That he failed to offer a positive course of action where none was to be seen, was perhaps more the part of wisdom than had he offered a panacea based upon pure speculation.

By the example of his will, Washington pointed the way to other slaveholders how their slaves might gradually be set free, even though the legislation which he had ever hoped for seemed distant.

## Summary

George Washington was born a slaveholder and the whole tradition in which he grew up sanctioned the righteousness and necessity of the slave system. He never attended a higher school or university and hence was not acquainted with the theoretical influences of the day, such as Locke and Rousseau which were making for democracy. Where he lived, slavery was universal and permitted by the Church as well as the Law. His early manhood was too strenuous for much reflective thougt on such problems. He made his living by owning and managing slaves on his estate.

When made Commander-in-Chief of the armies at Cambridge at the outbreak of the revolution, he didn't want to admit even free Negroes into the army. This was due to his background and early training. It was only because of necessity that he allowed Negroes to enlist.

When, with the Declaration of Independence, the theory of man's inalienable rights and of his equal creation became the common belief of all Americans, he was forced to be more lenient toward the Negroes. They were allowed to come into the army in battalions in Rhode Island and Washington himself thought they should be employed as wagon drivers in the South.

When the war was over and Washington had witnessed what fine soldiers the Negroes had made, he began to wonder if they were not something more than mere property. At this time he wrote to Lafayette that he would like to join him in his experiment with free Negroes. Bishop Asbury, when he visited Mount Vernon, had found him "against slavery." He had even written to a slave and addressed her as "Miss." He expressed the view that slavery ought to be abolished by degrees and by the law. To set the slaves free at once was, he thought, a dangerous proceeding.

His conflicting sentiments made him wish that the slaves would be free, but he was not radical enough to enter into a fight for their emancipation. At the Constitutional Convention, he remained silent because he didn't want to disturb the founding of the Union, which he held first in importance. Nor did he believe that the time was ripe to allow the matter to be debated in Congress. He referred to such attempts as the Quakers made, as "ill-timed." His slaves became a kind of property which he hated even to think about, and held with repugnance. Later in life he saw that unless legislative measures were taken for the gradual abolition of the system, there would be much mischief. His slaves represented so much of his entire estate that he couldn't afford to free them. He was "principled" against selling them because he didn't want to separate families or barter over them like cattle in a market. He stated that he wouldn't own a single slave in twelve months if he were not so "principled."

From his birth to his death he was a slaveholder

and controlled three hundred and seventeen slaves at the time of his death. His will continued to control their destinies even after his death. His belief in the importance of preserving the Union above all else, allowed him to remain officially silent regarding the danger of continuing the system.

# PART III.

# John Adams'
# Views on Negro Slavery

## John Adams (1735-1826)

While it is true that John Adams contributed little in behalf of the slave-trade, nevertheless as the follower of Washington to the presidency of the United States in 1796 his views merit consideration. He was born into one of New England's most prominent families, but failed to show the same love of democracy as did his illustrious kinsman, Samuel Adams (1722-1803). He believed in a natural aristocracy, an aristocracy of "talents and wealth" which should have control of the central government. His belief appears to have been sincere, but it is not hard to understand the unpopularity of such a point of view in early nineteenth century America. While at times he privately favored monarchy, he remained loyal to the Constitution and its form of representative government.

He was educated at Harvard and afterward practised law in Boston. During his early days he helped stir up Massachusetts for the Revolution. Later he was one of the delegates representing that colony in the Continental Congress. At the time that the Declaration of Independence was signed he was altogether in accord with Jefferson as to the validity of natural and inalienable rights. From the end of the Revolution in 1783 up until 1790 he seems to have undergone a change of heart. While he became a Federalist, insofar as he held the conservative view regarding the importance of property, pomp and ceremony, he never fully supported Hamilton's leanings in this direction.

Adams returned from his post as minister to Holland and became vice-president under Washington. He was elected on the Federalist ticket in 1796 as Washington's successor. His love of pomp and his many undemocratic blunders won many converts over to Jefferson's views. In the passage of the Alien and Sedition laws, which gave him the power to fine or imprison any persons who opposed the government, the knell of Federalism was sounded. He failed to be reelected, and lived for twenty-five years in retirement among his books. He was a practicable, unimaginative thinker who hated change and who deplored any change in the established order. He failed, not because of insincerity, but because his ideas were not progressive enough for the men of his generation. He faced the problems of the future with a good knowledge of history and a sound, practicable commonsense. He entertained no dreams for the reform or betterment of human nature and believed that as long as it remained as it was, it needed strong direction without too much liberty.

While believing in representative government, he wanted only the upper and middle classes to have voting power. The uneducated laborers and small farmers were unqualified in his estimation. On the other hand, he and Hamilton parted because he refused to recognize the financiers and the commercial class in general as America's natural aristocracy.

The slave problem lay dormant during his administration. It was supposed to have been settled by the Constitution and 1808 had been set as the year in which the importations of Negroes would end. There can be no doubt that he disliked slavery, although he was too conservative to take any direct action against it. Shortly before his death he wrote the following letter on the subject which leaves no doubt as to his sentiments:

"I have, through my whole life, held the practice of slavery in such abhorrence, that I have never owned a Negro or any other slave; though I have lived for many years in times when the practice was not disgraceful; when the best men in my vicinity thought it not inconsistent with their character; and when it cost me thousands of dollars for the labor and subsistence of free men, which I might have saved by the purchase of Negroes at times when they were very cheap." [1]

# PART IV.

# Thomas Jefferson's
# Views on Negro Slavery

## I.

### Why Jefferson's Views Are Important

Jefferson's views are important not only because of what he actually did and wished to do for the Negro slave, but also because he was perhaps the one early American statesman who was best equipped to understand and appreciate the theoretical dangers inherent in the institution. As a political philosopher he had the advantage, through education and a facility in foreign languages, of being in touch with the main trends of European political thought. Unlike his contemporary, Washington, he was not merely content with expressing dissatisfaction with slavery, but also took direct action against it upon more than one occasion. As a reformer, Jefferson never used the violent method of denunciation employed by so many later enthusiasts. There was too much of the English Squire in him to resort to combativeness. His conservative methods, and belief that social reforms were best brought about by legal means, closely resembled Washington's views. Although a descendant of one of the most socially prominent families in Virginia, he had a far deeper sympathy and understanding of the common people than Washington. He was always

85

strong in defense of the small farmer against government or class exploitation. Later, when under the guidance of Hamilton the evil vision of an aristocracy of wealth in control of the government lurked on the horizon, it was Jefferson who defended the common people. He believed in their ultimate intelligence and ability to govern themselves and he stood for the rights of the individual against state interference.

## II.

### Jefferson's Inheritance and Education

Thomas Jefferson was born on April 13, 1743, at Shadwell, the estate of his father, Peter Jefferson (1707-1757), located just above the junction of the Rivana and James rivers, on what was then the frontier of Western Virginia. The Jeffersons were a typical slaveholding Virginia family; perhaps one of the first to have settled in the colony. The name appears as early as 1619 among the list of members of the House of Burgesses, the first representative body to meet on the North American continent. On his mother's side he was related to the Randolphs, one of the most socially prominent families in the colony, of which he says, "they trace their pedigree far back in England and Scotland, to which let every one ascribe the faith and merit he chooses." [1] His father's family "came to this country from Wales, and from near the mountain of Snowdon, the highest in Great Britain." [2] Peter Jefferson was a Whig and a Democrat. On the frontier, equalitarian ideas were always popular. Here, man was in direct contact with nature and dependent upon his fellows for protection. People were far more interested in what a man was, than who his ancestors were. In the eastern part of the state, in the so-called tide-water region, the planters were far more imbued with English aristocratic ideas. Class distinctions meant more there than in the western or piedmont regions. We need only to contrast the conservative, complacent character of Washington with Jefferson's zeal for reform and his sympathetic understanding of the common people, to see the difference between these two sections of the state. There seems to be no doubt that Jefferson owes his early love of democracy to his western environment.

As far as family connections were concerned, Jefferson could easily have lived the life of the typical planter-aristocrat. His father died when the boy was fourteen and left him the lands on which he was born and lived. "He placed me at the English school at five years of age; and at the Latin at nine, where I continued until his death. My teacher, Mr. Douglas, a clergyman from Scotland, with the rudiments of the Latin and Greek languages, taught me the French; and on the death of my father, I went to the Reverend Mr. Maury, a correct classical scholar, with whom I continued two years; and then, to wit, in the spring of 1760, went to William and Mary College, where I continued two years." [3] The college was under the strict supervision of the Church of England. It offered "the grand old fortifying classical curriculum, that is to say . . . Latin, Greek, mathematics, moral philosophy, and a favorable view of the Christian faith as held by the Church of England." [4] Jefferson had what might be termed a Scotch education. He went from the hands of one Scotchman to another. "It was my great good fortune, and what probably fixed the destinies of my life, that Dr. William Small of Scotland, was then professor of Mathematics, a man profound in most of the useful branches of science, with a happy talent for communication, correct and gentlemanly manners, and an enlarged and liberal mind. He, most happily for me, became soon attached to me, and made me his daily companion when not engaged in the school; and from his conversation I got my first views of the expansion of science, and of the system of things in which we are placed." [5] Upon Dr. Small's return to Europe in 1762, he arranged with his friend George Wythe, to take young Jefferson in as a student of law, "Mr. Wythe continued to be my faithful and beloved mentor in youth, and my most affectionate friend through life." [6] It was this George Wythe who was so eager to see laws passed for the abolition of slavery, that when this legislation was delayed, he became impatient and gave all his slaves their freedom without asking whether by so doing, he was acting for their own best welfare. That Wythe's idea on Negro slavery had a strong influence upon young Jefferson cannot be doubted. In 1767, Wythe introduced Jefferson as a member of the bar where he continued as a lawyer "until the Revolution shut up the courts of justice." [7]

## III.

### First Effort to Emancipate the Slaves

Jefferson first entered public service as a Justice of the Peace. A few years later, in 1769, he was elected a member of the Virginia House of Burgesses in which body he remained until he became a member of the Continental Congress in 1775.

Young Jefferson's first legislative effort in the House

of Burgesses was a failure. It gives us, nevertheless, an insight as to how important he considered the problem of Negro slavery, even at this early date. That his first legislative effort should have been one which would have permitted slave masters to have freed their slaves, shows the relative importance of this question in his mind. In his "Autobiography," (a short summary of his life, written at the age of seventy-seven), he says, "I made one effort in the body (the House of Burgesses) for the permission of the emancipation of slaves, which was rejected: and indeed during the regal government, nothing liberal could expect success. Our minds were circumscribed within narrow limits, by an habitual belief that it was our duty to be subordinate to the mother country in all matters of government . . . and even to observe a bigoted intolerance for all religions but her. The difficulties with our representatives were of habit and despair, not of reflection and conviction." [1] This method of calm "reflection and conviction" was employed by Jefferson throughout his whole life in reaching political opinions. His famous colleague, Washington, depended far more on his inherited traditions and feelings. But Jefferson had the courage of his conviction when he thought they would lead to some benefit for his fellow men. Perhaps the failure of his first attempt to free the slaves of Virginia by law, showed him how slowly things must move in the realm of politics where feeling and self-interest are usually stronger than reason and theory. It is a mistake to think that this effort of Jefferson's was inspired solely by a pity for the condition of the slaves, for we must remember that Virginia had too many slaves at the time and it was the increase in their numbers which not only filled their masters with terror at the thought of possible insurrection, but which also was slowly bringing many of them to economic ruin, as in the case of Washington.

## IV.

### Instructions to the Virginia Delegation

In the summer of 1774, the several counties of the State of Virginia elected deputies to meet at Williamsburg to consider the state of the colony, and particularly to appoint delegates to a general Congress. Philadelphia was appointed for the place, and the 5th of September for the time of the meeting.[1] Jefferson returned to his home at Monticello and a general election was held by the people to choose their delegates to the first Continental Congress. "Being elected one for my own county (Albermarle), I prepared a draught of instructions to be given to the delegate . . ."[2] Setting out for Williamsburg, Jefferson "was taken ill of a dysentery on the road and was unable to proceed." He sent on, therefore, to Williamsburg, two copies of his draught. We learn that one copy was laid "on the table for perusal. It was generally read by the members, approved by many, though *thought too bold* for the present state of things; but they printed it in pamphlet form, under the title of 'A Summary View of the Rights of British America.'"[3]

In a study of Jefferson's view on the problem of Negro slavery, there is, of course, no place for an analysis of this document which foreshadows in many respects the whole political philosophy which he afterwards wrote into the Declaration of Independence. The pamphlet, in general, attempted to show that "the relation between Great Britain and these colonies was exactly the same as that of England and Scotland, after the accession of James, and until the union, the same as her present relations with Hanover, having the same political chief, but no other necessary political connection; and that our migration from England to this country gave her no more rights over us, than the migration of the Danes and Saxons gave to the present authorities of the mother country, over England."[4]

In this pamphlet we see Jefferson as the lawyer and student of English constitutional history, deeply concerned with the *rights* of America. In the Declaration of Independence, this appeal to *rights* was re-enforced by making an appeal to the "natural" and "inalienable rights" of man over the power of any state. Jefferson first wanted legal separation. That having been denied, he turned philosopher and employed the theory of natural rights to justify the American Revolution. How he came by these ideas we shall attempt to show on a later page. What concerns us here is, that in this remarkable pamphlet, Jefferson's first printed work, we find him pointing out to his Majesty George III, the "deviations from the line of duty" with regard to the abolition of domestic slavery and the slave trade.

"For the most trifling reasons, and, sometimes for no conceivable reason at all, his Majesty has rejected laws of the most salutary tendency, The abolition of domestic slavery is the great object of desire in those colonies, where it was, unhappily introduced in their infant state. But previous to the enfranchisement of the slaves we have, it is necessary to exclude all further importations from Africa. Yet our repeated attempts to effect this by prohibitions, and by imposing duties which might amount to a prohibition, have been hitherto defeated by his Majesty's negative; thus preferring the immediate advantages of a few British corsairs to the lasting interests of the American states, and to the rights of human nature, deeply wounded by this infamous practise." [5]

It is not hard to understand why this document failed to arouse the unanimous approval of all the delegates when we consider that the majority were slaveowners, whose plantations depended upon slave-labor for their support.

## V.

### The Declaration of Independence [1]

It would be a great mistake if I should give the impression that Jefferson was mainly concerned with the question of Negro slavery. In fact the very opposite was the case, and the hardest task of the author is to ignore the many other important reforms with which Jefferson was at the time concerned. A study of his views on the slave question must necessarily omit most of the other reforms and measures which mark him as America's first great political philosopher. There are, however, parts of the Declaration of Independence and of his Virginia Reforms, which although not exclusively concerned with slavery, yet throw such a light upon Jefferson's whole philosophy, that they should not be ignored.

In the Declaration of Independence which was largely his work, although the aged Franklin, John Adams, Roger Sherman and Robert Livingston were members of the committee, we find Jefferson taking a decidedly defensive view of the Revolution in compliance with the legalistic ideas of the time. The traditional view, held even by most Americans, is that Jefferson laid down the philosophical principles upon which American democracy was founded, with clear prophetic vision in the Declaration of Independence. That these principles were those which later took the world by storm and played a large part in bringing about the French Revolution is believed by many. Let us examine the Declaration objectively to see how far these beliefs are true.

There can be no doubt that the form of the document is typically legal. It begins with a preamble which is followed by a long list of charges held to be contrary to the British constitution and ends in a judgment against the offender. The document employs the typical legal language of the day.

Nor does Jefferson appeal to the world alone to justify his principles. His appeal is primarily to the law and is made to justify America's *right* to withdraw from Great Britain.

"We, therefore, the representatives of the United States of America in general Congress assembled... solemnly publish and declare that these united colonies are, *and of right ought to be*, free and independent states...." [2]

It is an attempt to place the blame for the Revolution upon Great Britain and to show that the American colonies had a right to withdraw, i.e., that Great Britain is the aggressor and that America can do nothing else but revolt under the circumstances.

Let us look at that part of the Declaration which contains the philosophical ideas which are supposed to have been borrowed from European sources.

"We hold these truths to be self-evident that all

men are created equal, that they are endowed by their creator with inherent and inalienable rights, that among these are life, liberty and the pursuit of happiness; that to secure these rights governments are instituted among men deriving their just powers from the consent of the governed; that whenever any government becomes destructive of these ends, it is the right of the people to alter or to abolish it, and to institute new government, laying its foundation on such principles and organizing its powers in such form as to them shall seem most likely to effect their happiness."

If, then, it is a self-evident truth that all men are created equal, are not the Negroes entitled to the same life, liberty and pursuit of happiness as other men? That is the natural question one would ask. How could a body of men subscribing to these high sentiments tolerate slavery. How could Jefferson continue as a slaveholder if he really took his own words seriously?

To answer these questions we must bear in mind that when this document was written the general sentiment in all the colonies was against slavery. Everyone thought it would only be a matter of time before emancipation would take place according to law. There was no division among the States such as slave states and free states, Northern or Southern. All these distinctions arose later and had their grounds in the economic, geographic, climatic peculiarities of the two sections. Besides, we must remember that this document was written in a great political crisis, when the colonies were seeking to justify their right to revolt. It is quite possible that Jefferson, when he penned these lofty sentiments, was so stirred by a

broad view of the rights of all men, that he threw
in this Lockian argument as a bit of ornamental philosophy with which to strengthen his legal arguments.
It seems more probable, however, that he was convinced of the truth of the doctrine of natural and
inalienable rights and wished to lay it down as a
principle which would serve as a model for the future
government and perhaps help to bring about the slave
emancipation which he so much desired.

Jefferson had a practical sense which served as a
check on vain excursions into abstract thought. This
is one ground for thinking that the "self-evident"
principles, so near to those of Locke, appearing in
the Declaration of Independence, were, perhaps, not
arrived at by his own reasoning process. He was
singularly prejudiced against metaphysics and all spec-
ulative thinking. "I revolt against all metaphysical
reading... some acquaintance with the operations of
the mind is worth acquiring. But any one of the
writers suffice for that." He then recommends Locke,
Hartley, Stewart, Brown, Reid, Tracy and others as
being equally good. These "dreams," he tells us,
"vanish in vapor," and adds that "the business of life
is with matter. That gives us tangible results... from
metaphysical speculations I have never seen one
useful result." [3]

The question arises as to whether these "self-
evident" principles were originated by Jefferson or not,
and if not, from what sources they came. Luckily the
best answer to this question is given by Jefferson himself. He tells us that in writing the document his purpose was "not to find new principles, or new arguments, never before thought of, not merely to say
things which had never before been said; but to place
before mankind the common sense of the subject,

in terms so plain and firm as to command their assent.... Neither aiming at originality of principles of sentiments, nor yet copied from any particular and previous writing, it was *intended to be an expression of the American mind. ... All its authority rests then upon the harmonizing sentiments of the day*, whether expressed in conversation, in letters, printed essays or the elementary books of public right, as Aristotle, Cicero, Locke, Sidney, etc." [4]

Otto Vossler, in the work quoted above, says that whoever today reads in the above quotation a statement that the government is no greater than the people, or whoever sees in it the doctrine of equal votes for all; Republican principles, etc., reads into it ideas which had no meaning in 1776. Such a reading of it is unconsciously influenced by a knowledge of the French Revolution and later developments.[5]

The common consent of modern research seems to be that the "harmonizing sentiments of the day" were not only those of Locke[6] but also of the English body of common law; surely not those of French revolutionary thought. It was only later that these principles were identified with Rousseau and French thought. It is well to remember that the French philosophers themselves borrowed the doctrine of inalienable rights from Locke, and that Voltaire acknowledged the debt openly.

There have been extensive studies made into the question of how much Jefferson borrowed, and how much was original, in the philosophy of the Declaration of Independence. Gilbert Chinard thinks it closely resembles the language used by George Mason in "The Virginia Bill of Rights" written in 1774.[7] Becker, another authority on Jefferson, points out its resemblance to a pamphlet written by James Wilson in 1770.[8] The following paragraph gives an excellent summary of the whole question:

"The hunt for a speech or pamphlet which Jefferson might have copied has failed. Everything has been ransacked. His masterpiece turns out to be just as original, or just as hackneyed as the Magna Charta. It was the product of a political genius working, under the presence and passionate inspiration of a glorious moment in his country's history, for a cause on which he had embarked heart and soul, life and fortune. If he had brought with him his library from Monticello, and had consulted his favorite political authors, Coke, Sydney, Locke, and the rest of them, for ideas and phrases, the thing would have been a failure. It was the fruit of well-digested reading, long and strenuous controversy, not a copy nor an imitation of the past, but a new effervescence of spirit, an expression, in language characteristic of the man and the times, of a new policy." [9]

In the Declaration of Independence, the following paragraph pertaining to slavery and the slave trade was prepared by Jefferson in his first draft of the document:

"He (George III) has waged cruel war against human nature itself, violating its most sacred rights of life and liberty in the persons of a distant people who never offended him, captivating and carrying them into slavery in another hemisphere, or to incur miserable death in their transportation thither. This piratical warfare, the opprobium of infidel powers, is the warfare of the Christian king of Great Briton determined to keep open a market where men should be bought and sold, he has prostituted his negative for suppressing every legislative attempt to prohibit or to restrain this execrable commerce. And that this assemblage of horrors might want no fact of distinguished die, he is now exciting those very people to rise in arms among us, and to purchase that liberty of which he has deprived them, by murdering the people on whom he also obtruded them; thus paying off former crimes committed against the *liberties* of one people, with crimes which he urges them to commit against the lives of another." [10]

This paragraph was struck out, Jefferson tells us, in compliance to South Carolina and Georgia, who had never attempted to restrain the importation of slaves, and who on the contrary still wished it to continue. "Our Northern brethren also, I believe, felt a little tender under those censures; for though their people had very few slaves themselves, yet they had been pretty considerable carriers of them to others." [11]

Writing again about this slavery paragraph which was stricken out of the Declaration of Independence, Jefferson says that the measure was disapproved "by some Southern gentlemen, whose reflections were not yet matured to the full abhorrence of that traffic."[12] This was the first evidence of a rupture which increased until it was finally settled by the Civil War which raged in America from 1861 to 1865.

It is perhaps better that the above paragraph was not allowed to remain in the document, for it seems rather unfair that George the Third should be held solely responsible for American slavery. On the other hand had a strong disapproval of the slave trade and slavery been included in the Declaration of Independence, it would have made the way much easier toward final emancipation via legal methods. This was Jefferson's third attempt to strike at the wrongs of slavery. It must be acknowledged that there were no other important statesmen, not even Washington himself, who had the courage to risk his position of popular favor or his political future in an attempt to remedy this evil.

## VI.

### Jefferson's Virginia Reforms

With his reputation as the author of the Declaration of Independence, Jefferson in the summer of 1776 and at the age of thirty-three, was marked out as the possible leader of the civil administration. It came as a surprise to many, when he resigned his seat in Congress and took a seat in the Virginia House of Representatives in October of the same year. His wife was not in good health and he wanted to be near her and the children during the uncertainties of the approaching war. He was also somewhat disgusted with the amount of useless debate in the Continental Congress.

"If the present Congress errs in too much talking, how can it be otherwise in a body to which the people send one hundred and fifty lawyers, whose trade it is to question everything, yield nothing, and talk by the hour?" [1]

Besides his disgust for the wranglings of Congress, he realized the great need of reforming the antiquated laws of his beloved Virginia. The criminal laws were not fit for a civilized state. Witches and heretics could be burned to death, while Baptists, Quakers and Unitarians could be punished by long prison terms for opposing the Established Church. [2]

When the Legislature of the new State of Virginia opened, Jefferson proposed a measure for reorganizing the courts of justice. This was passed. The next day he introduced a bill to do away with the old English custom that the eldest son should inherit the greater part of the estate, i.e., the law of primogeniture. This was finally passed. His next bill did away with the death penalty except in cases of treason and murder. With all the zeal of a reformer, Jefferson set about to write laws for the education of the whole people. There should be public schools of different grades established so that a poor man's son would have the same chance of advancing in education as a rich man's son, he believed. This bill failed because Jefferson had put the cost of such schools on the inhabitants of the different counties according to their taxable capacity, the burden of which they were unwilling to bear.

It is the fifth of these reforms, the one pertaining to slavery, with which we are most concerned. Jefferson tells us in his Autobiography:

"The bill on the subject of slaves, was a mere digest of the existing laws, without any intimation of a plan for a future and general emancipation. It was thought better that this should be kept back, and attempted only by way of amendment, whenever the bill should be brought on. The principles of the amendment, however, were agreed upon, that is to say, the freedom of all born after a certain day, and deportation at a proper age. But it was found that the public would not yet bear the proposition, nor will it bear it even at this day.[3] Yet the day is not distant when it must bear and adopt it, or worse will follow. Nothing is more certainly written in the book of fate, than that these people are to be free; nor is it less certain that the two races, equally free, cannot live in the same government. Nature, habit, opinion have drawn indelible lines of distinction between them. It is still in our power to direct the process of emancipation and deportation, peaceably, and in such slow degree, as that the evil will wear off insensibly, and their place be, *pari passu*, filled up by free white laborers. If, on the contrary, it is left to force itself on, human nature must shudder at the prospect held up. We should in vain look for an example in the Spanish deportation or deletion of the Moors. This precedent would fall short of our case."

But the most famous of the reforms, the one by which the name of Jefferson will live the longest, was "A Bill for Establishing Religious Freedom." [4] It is appropriate to say a word about it here to show that Jefferson's love of liberty in every sphere was genuine and not political. It cannot be compared in form to Milton's *Areopagitica* although in content it went beyond Milton and even Locke. It was a passionate plea for real toleration; not merely conventional toleration. His aim was to found a real freedom of conscience based upon the law of the land. The statute declared "that our civil rights have no dependence on our religious opinions, more than our opinions in physics or geometry." . . . "It is time enough for the rightful purposes of civil government for its officers to interfere when principles break out into overt acts against peace and good order . . . truth is great and will prevail if left to herself." The bill ends with the resolution, "That no man shall be compelled to frequent or support any religious worship, place, or ministry whatsoever. . . ." "The rights hereby asserted, are of the natural rights of mankind. . . ."

The Presbyterians and other dissenters tried to get state support for their sects in 1784 after Jefferson had sailed for France. Their idea was that there should be a general assessment on the taxpayers for "teachers of the Christian Religion" but they failed in spite of the fact that George Washington and Patrick Henry backed them.

Jefferson sincerely wished to better the world, but unlike most reformers, he wished to do so only on the condition that the liberties of others would not be interfered with. In 1800 he wrote that he had sworn upon the altar of God, eternal hostility against every form of tyranny over the mind of man.

## VII.

### The "Notes on Virginia"

In June, 1781, Jefferson, while confined to his room, began to write his first and only book.[1] He had been asked a number of questions about Virginia by the Marquis of Marbois, then a member of the French legation in Philadelphia. Jefferson, who had always been in the habit of jotting down anything on paper which he thought might be of value later, had a great deal of information pertaining to his native state. It occurred to him to write a book, using the Marquis' questions as chapter headings, and thus bring into order this mass of loose material. The book was finished the following year, but remained unpublished owing to the high cost of such work. In 1784, when Jefferson arrived in Paris as Minister of the United States, he found that his book could be printed at about one-fourth the cost of American prices, so he ordered two hundred copies printed, giving it the title "Notes on Virginia."

The book is encyclopaedic in its extent, treating on one page the geography and weather of Virginia and on the next, its religious and educational reforms. Jefferson accepts no responsibility for the plan of the work, as it attempts only to answer the twenty-three questions put to him by Marbois. He sent the book only to a few of his close friends, after it was first openly published in 1787.[2] A miserable French translation was also published by Abbé Morellet. In the following letter to Chastellux written in 1785, Jefferson explains why he did not want to make the contents of his book known in America:

"The strictures on slavery and on the constitution of Virginia . . . are the parts I do not wish to have made public, at least till I know whether their publication would do most harm or good. It is possible that in my own country these strictures might produce an irritation which would indispose the people towards the two great objects I have in view, that is emancipation of their slaves and the settlement of their constitution on a firmer and more permanent basis."[3]

It is in the chapter entitled "Query XIV" that he discusses Negroes and Negro slavery. He begins by informing us that many of the laws which were in force during the monarchy have been found inconsistent with republicanism, and that a committee to revise the whole code has been undertaken by three gentlemen.[4] According to his opinion, the most remarkable alteration proposed is, besides a law to establish religious freedom on the broadest bottom, a law to emancipate all slaves born after the passing of the act.

We learn that all Negro slave children shall, under the new law, "continue with their parents to a certain age, then to be brought up, at the public expense, to tillage, arts, or sciences according to their geniuses, till the females should be eighteen, and the males twenty-one years of age, when they should be colonized to such place as the circumstances of the time should render most proper."

While wishing for emancipation, Jefferson never entertained the idea that the Negroes should be absorbed by the white population of America or even be admitted to an equal footing in the state. His idea was to colonize them, "sending them out with arms, implements of household and of handicraft arts, seeds, pairs of useful animals, etc., to declare them a free and independent people, and extend to them our alliance and protection, till they have acquired strength; and to send vessels at the same time to other parts of the world for an equal number of white inhabitants; to induce them to migrate hither, proper encouragements were to be proposed." Little did Jefferson suspect how readily white settlers would soon be flocking to America from the old world!

Jefferson gives us his reasons why the United States should not attempt to incorporate the blacks into the state. He believed that the two races could never live peaceably side by side. The "deep-rooted prejudices entertained by the whites," as well as the "ten thousand recollections, by the blacks, of the injuries they have sustained" . . . "distinctions which nature has made; and many other circumstances, will divide us into parties, and produce convulsions, which will probably never end but in the extermination of our or of the other race."

Having disposed of the political objections, he undertakes to point out the physical differences between the two races. The first of these differences is, of course, that of color. "Whether the black of the Negro resides in the reticular membrane between the skin and the scarf-skin, or in the scarf-skin itself; whether it proceeds from the color of the blood, the color of the bile, or from that of some other secretion, the difference is fixed in nature, and is as real as if its seat and cause were better known to us."

Jefferson, then, attempts to show that the white race is more beautiful than the black. He asks us whether the blushes; those "fine mixtures of red and white" which lend to the "expressions of every passion" in the white race, are not superior to the "eternal monotony . . . that immovable veil of black which covers the emotions of the other race?" We must recognize that the whites besides having "flowing hair" and "a more elegant symmetry of form" are considered by the blacks themselves as the more beautiful, If then, "superior beauty, is thought worthy attention in the propagation of our horses, dogs, and other domestic animals; why not in that of man?"

Further, he points out that there are other distinctions which prove a difference in the races. Among these are, "less hair on the face and body." "They secrete less by the kidneys; and more by the glands of the skin, which gives them a very strong and disagreeable odor." "They seem to require less sleep." "They are at least as brave, and more adventuresome than the whites. But this may perhaps proceed from a want of forethought." "They are more ardent after their female; but love seems to them to be more an eager desire, than a tender delicate mixture of sentiment and sensation." "Their griefs are transient." "In general, their existence appears to participate more of sensations than reflection." ". . . In memory they are equal to the whites; in reason much inferior . . . in imagination they are dull, tasteless, and anomalous."

Jefferson then warns of the danger of forming hasty judgments and adds that it will be right to make great allowances for the difference of condition, of education, of conversation, of the sphere in which they move.

Reminding us that while the majority of the blacks have been confined to their own society, he finds it surprising how little those who have enjoyed close association with the whites, have benefited by it. The American Indians, with none of these advantages, "often carve figures on their pipes not destitute of design or merit." This shows that the Indians have "a germ in their minds which only wants cultivation. They (the Indians) astonish you with strokes of the most sublime oratory; such as prove their reason and sentiment strong. But never yet could I find that a black had uttered a thought above the level of plain narration; never saw even an elementary trait of painting or sculpture." In music, Jefferson considers the blacks more generally gifted than the whites with acute ears for tune and time. He reminds us that they have been "capable of imagining" the musical instrument known as the banjo, but doubts whether they will be equal to the composition of a more extensive run of melody, or of complicated harmony.

Commenting on the lack of poetry among the blacks, he reminds us that misery is often the parent of poetry. "Among the blacks is misery enough, God knows, but no poetry." Love is also "the peculiar oestrum of the poet." But love only "kindles the senses" of the Negro and not his imagination. "Religion," he says, "has produced a Phyllis Wheatley;[5] but it could not produce a poet. The compositions published under her name are below the dignity of criticism. The heroes of the Dunciad are to her, as Hercules to the author of that poem."

Among the Romans, the conditions of the slaves was "much more deplorable" than the American slaves. The sexes were kept separate in Rome, because "to raise a child cost the master more than to buy one." On the other hand, in America, "slaves multiply as fast as the free inhabitants," . . . "whereas in Rome we are told," Cato, on "a principle of economy, always sold his sick and superannuated slaves."[6] American slaves cannot count this "among the injuries and insults they receive." "With the Romans, the regular method of taking evidence of their slaves was under torture. Here it has been thought better never to resort to their evidence. When a master was murdered, all his slaves, in the same house, or within hearing, were condemned to death. Here punishment falls on the guilty only, and as precise proof is required against him as against a freeman." It was because the Roman slaves were white that among them were "rare artists," scientists and "tutors to their masters' children." "Epictetus, Terence and Phaedrus, were slaves." The difference is not then of condition only, but of nature. "Whether further observation will or will not verify the conjecture, that nature has been less bountiful to them (the blacks) in the endowments of the head, I believe that in those of the heart she will be found to have done them justice."

He defends the Negro against that disposition to theft with which they have been branded. He explains that this must be ascribed to their situation, and not to any depravity of the moral sense and that the man in whose favor no laws of property exist, probably feels himself less bound to respect those made in favor of others.

Jefferson hesitated in putting the Negroes on the same level as white men. He takes the role of the scientist and warns us that we cannot say definitely that the blacks are inferior until they have been the subject of serious observation over a long period of time. We cannot "degrade a whole race of men from the work in the scale of beings which their creator may perhaps have given them. . . . I advance it, therefore, as a suspicion only, that the blacks, whether originally a distinct race, or made distinct by time and circumstance, are inferior to the whites in the endowment both of body and mind. It is not against experience to suppose that different species of the same genus, or varieties of the same species, may possess different qualifications. Will not a lover of natural history then, one who views the degradations in all races of animals with the eye of philosophy, excuse an effort to keep those in the department of man as distinct as nature has formed them."

It seems the proper place to call attention to a letter which Jefferson addressed to M. Grégoire, Evêque et Sénateur, from the White House in Washington in February, 1809, just before the expiration of his second term as President of the United States. It appears that Grégoire had read Jefferson's "Notes on Virginia" but could not agree with his suspicion that the blacks were inferior to the whites in body and mind.

"My doubts were the result of personal observation on the limited sphere of my own state, when the opportunities for the development of their genius were not favorable, and those of exercising it still less so. I expressed them, therefore, with great hesitation; but, *whatever be their degree of talent, it is no measure of their rights.* Because Sir Isaac Newton was superior to others in understanding, he was not, therefore, lord of the person or property of others. On this subject they are gaining daily in the opinions of nations, and hopeful advances are making towards their re-establishment on an equal footing with the other colors of the human family. I pray you, therefore, to accept my thanks for the many instances you have enabled me to observe of respectable intelligence in that race of men, which cannot fail to have effect in hastening the day of their relief." [7]

In the above letter we find Jefferson rather apologetic for the doubts he once cast upon Negro intelligence in his Notes. But something altogether new appears in the above letter, namely his insistence on the *rights* of the blacks. Back in 1784, when the Notes were first published, Jefferson was not yet ready to concede that the Negro had rights. Now in 1809 he finds "hopeful advances."

Speaking of the difficulties which stand in the way of emancipation, he emphasizes those "of color and *perhaps* of faculty." While many masters would like to free their slaves and vindicate the liberty of human nature they are at the same time "anxious also to preserve its dignity and beauty." That is why, in answer to the question "What is to be done with them?" they "join themselves in opposition with those who are actuated by sordid avarice only." In Rome, a slave could be emancipated "without staining the blood of his master," but in America a situation exists that has no precedent in history and that is why the "Negro slave in America must be removed beyond the reach of mixture."

It is a great mistake to think that Jefferson's opposition to slavery was grounded in pure altruism. In a later chapter of the Notes[8] we find his well-considered reasons for such opposition. He objects to slavery because it is degrading as much so for the master as for the slave. Besides being bad for the morals of the people, it destroys "their industry."

"There must doubtless be an unhappy influence on the manners of our people produced by the existence of slavery among us. The whole commerce between master and slave is a perpetual exercise of the most boisterous passions, the most unremitting despotism on the one part, and degrading submissions on the other. Our children see this, and learn to imitate it; for man is an imitative animal. . . . The man must be a prodigy who can retain his manners and morals undepraved by such circumstances. . . . With the morals of the people their industry also is destroyed. For in a warm climate, no man will labor for himself who can make another labor for him. This is so true, that of the proprietors of slaves a very small proportion indeed are ever seen to labor. And can the liberties of a nation be thought secure when we have removed their only firm basis, a conviction in the minds of the people that these liberties are the gift of God? That they are not to be violated but with his wrath?"

Since the Revolution a change is noted. "The spirit of the masters is abating, that of the slave rising from the dust . . . the way I hope preparing . . . for a total emancipation" and that this shall be "with the consent of the masters, rather than by their extirpation."
Jefferson, the Agrarian and Physiocrat, was ever firm in his belief that America should remain an agri-

cultural country. He saw great danger in any great growth of industry. Not only would a proletariat class be created in the North, but also slavery would doubtless become then a permanent institution in the South. If industry spread and slave labor became more skilled and productive, he saw that there would be little hope for emancipation. He was always looking for a graceful and timely way to bring this about without causing slave or slaveholder too much economic hardship.

Before he left Paris in 1788, he wrote to a certain M. Warville, "you know that nobody wishes more ardently to see an abolition, not only of the slave trade, but of the condition of slavery; and certainly, nobody will be more willing to encounter every sacrifice for that object." [9]

## VIII.

### The Sack of Monticello and Rochefoucauld's Visit

Writing from Paris in 1788, Jefferson told a friend, how seven years before, his estate, Monticello, had been plundered.

In 1781 Lord Cornwallis, himself, "destroyed all my growing crops of corn and tobacco. He burned all my barns containing the same articles of the last year, having first taken what corn he wanted; he used, as was to be expected, all my stock of cattle, sheep and hogs for the sustenance of his army. . . . He carried off also about thirty slaves. *Had this been to give them freedom, he would have done right*; but it was to consign them to inevitable death from the small pox and putrid fever,[1] then raging in his camp." [2]

The above passage is remarkable in that it gives us Jefferson's definite statement that had Cornwallis carried off the slaves with the purpose of setting them free, he would have "done right." We may ask why it was that Jefferson didn't free his slaves if he thought it was right? The reason was that Jefferson didn't believe in setting slaves free in the United States. He never believed that the two races could live peaceably side by side, and his solution to the problem was to colonize the Negroes in Africa or some other distant place "beyond the reach of mixture." [8] This letter, then, must be taken to mean that had Cornwallis carried off the thirty slaves with the intention of setting them free, in some distant land, he would have "done right." That Jefferson was ready to acknowledge this principle in the face of such a severe loss of property, shows his fairness and the strong belief in the natural rights of humanity, which he always upheld.

In the same letter, Jefferson describes what the British army did in the Southern States in 1781:

"Lord Cornwallis' character in England would forbid the belief that he shared the plunder; but that his table was served with the plate thus pillaged from private houses, can be proved by many hundred eye-witnesses. From an estimate I made at the time, on the best information I could collect, I supposed the state of Virginia lost, under Lord Cornwallis' hands, that year, about thirty thousand slaves; and that of these, about twenty-seven thousand died of the small pox and camp fever, and the rest were partly sent to the West Indies, and exchanged for rum, sugar, coffee and fruit, and partly sent to New York, from whence they went, at the peace, either to Nova Scotia or England. From this last place, I believe they have been lately sent to Africa. History will never relate the horrors committed by the British army in the Southern States of America. They raged in Virginia six months only . . . when they were all taken prisoners . . . I suppose their whole devastations during those six months, amounted to about three millions sterling." [4]

In the summer of 1796 the Duc de la Rochefoucauld-Liancourt paid him a week's visit at Monticello. The duke seemed much impressed by the civil way in which Jefferson managed his slaves, and gives us the following picture of life on the estate:

"I found him (Jefferson) in the midst of the harvest, from which the scorching heat of the sun does not prevent his attendance. His Negroes are clothed, and treated as well as white servants could be . . . every article is made on his farm; his Negroes are cabinet makers, carpenters, masons, bricklayers, smiths, etc. The children, he employs in a nail factory, which yields already a considerable profit. The young and old Negresses spin for the clothing of the rest. He animates them by rewards and distinctions. . . ."

When the war of 1812 cut off European imports, Jefferson installed various machines "costing $150 only, and worked by two women and two girls." [5] These, we are told, furnished some two thousand yards of cloth which was needed each year to clothe Monticello's masters and slaves.

Like Washington, Jefferson was a close observer of his slaves. There are many entries in his "Farm Book" as follows:

"Johnny Hemings began the body of a Landau Jan. 12 and finished it this day, being nine weeks, 5 days. He had not more help from Lewis than made up for his interruptions. The smith's work employed the two smiths perhaps 1-3 of the same time." [6]

Another item reads:

"Johnny Hem and Lewis began a dressing table and finished it in exactly 6 weeks of which 4 weeks was such dreadful weather, that, even within doors, nothing like full work could be done." [7]

Nock points out that one of the great problems of all persons who owned slaves was to find useful occupations for the children; occupations that would not only keep them out of mischief but could be turned into profit. Jefferson's plan was "Children till 10 years old to serve as nurses; from 10 to 16 the boys make nails, the girls spin; at 16 go into the ground (on the farm) or learn trades." [8] An estimate on "the actual work of the autumn of 1794" shows that one-fourth of the profit at the nail factory was lost through wastage. This gives us some idea of the inefficiency of slave labor. Nock asks us "what better could be done with these boys? They could not be effectively disciplined. They could not be discharged; they were slave children, permanently on one's hands. It was to no purpose to try to educate them beyond their slave-status; and even if one killed them off, their place would be taken almost immediately by others precisely like them." [9]

It was this endless multiplication of the slaves, together with their inefficiency as laborers which was gradually driving many Virginia planters toward impoverishment. It would be unfair to say that such arguments as the "inalienable rights" of all men to life, liberty and the pursuit of happiness or the pronouncement that "all men are created equal" had no effect upon eighteenth-century Americans. It is, however, necessary to know that there were strong practical economic reasons against slavery as well as humane and theoretical grounds for opposing it.

## IX

### The Ordinance of 1787, Act of 1807 and the Missouri Compromise

In 1784, Jefferson was made chairman of a committee in Congress to work out a plan for the government of the vast territory which lies north of the 31st parallel and which is now divided into the states of Kentucky, Tennessee, Mississippi and Alabama. The report contained a clause to the effect that after the year 1800 there should be neither slavery nor involuntary servitude in any of the said states. It is a great pity that this clause failed by only one vote. It certainly would have checked the growth of the Slave Power and might have prevented the Civil War. Writing about it soon afterwards, Jefferson said, "the voice of a single individual . . . would have prevented this abominable crime from spreading itself over the new country. Thus we see the fate of millions unborn hanging on the tongue of one man, and Heaven was silent in that awful moment! But it is to be hoped it will not always be silent, and that the friends to the rights of human nature will in the end prevail." [1]

It is needless to say that Jefferson lost many Southern friends by this constant fight against slavery. Three years later, in 1787, an ordinance was passed which prohibited slavery north of the Ohio river. This was done while Jefferson was in France, but it can be imagined how pleased he was with the result. This territory, out of which the States of Ohio, Indiana, Illinois, Michigan and Wisconsin have since been carved, belonged to the United States as a nation. It was known as the National Domain and was governed over directly by the Continental Congress. Slavery was prohibited "forever" within its limits. Thus the Ohio river became the boundary between freedom and slavery and all the states north of it came into the Union as free states.

Jefferson was elected President of the United States in 1801 and by far the greatest event of his first administration was the purchase of a great tract of land from France, lying west of the Mississippi River and extending from the Gulf of Mexico to what is now the Dominion of Canada. The price paid was fifteen million dollars and it more than doubled the territory of the United States. At first, the question arose as to whether the purchase was constitutional, but it seemed such a good buy for the future of the nation that there was little opposition to it.

In 1805 Jefferson was again elected President and during his second term, in 1808, the importation of slaves into the United States became illegal. It will be remembered that Congress had, by way of compromise with a few of the Southern States, set the year 1808 as the limit of the slave trade. As a matter of fact, this traffic was secretly continued for a number of years afterwards. It was thought by many that with the end of the slave-trade, the institution of slavery itself would not be long in dying out. But this was just the opposite of what actually happened.

President Jefferson, in a message to Congress on December 2, 1806, said:

"I congratulate you, fellow citizens, on the approach

of the period at which you may interpose your authority constitutionally to withdraw the citizens of the United States from all further participation in those violations of human rights which have been so long continued on the unoffending inhabitants of Africa, and which the morality, the reputation and the best interests of our country, have long been eager to proscribe. Although no law you may pass can take prohibitory effect till the first day of the year one thousand eight hundred and eight, yet the intervening period is not too long to prevent, by timely notice, expeditions which cannot be completed before that day." [2]

A great debate took place in the Senate and in the House of Representatives which finally ended in the enactment of the famous Act of 1807. The first question dealt with was: How shall illegally imported Africans be disposed of? This question was finally settled as follows:

"Section 4. . . . And neither the importer, nor any person or persons claiming from or under him, shall hold any right or title whatsoever to any Negro, mulatto, or person of color, nor to the service or labor thereof, who may be imported or brought within the United States, or territories thereof, in violation of this law, but the same shall remain subject to any regulations not contravening the provisions of this act, which the Legislatures of the several States or Territories at any time hereafter may make, for disposing of any such Negro, mulatto, or person of color." [3]

The second question debated was: How shall violations be punished? The act settled it in the following manner:

"For equipping a slaver, a fine of $20,000 and forfeiture of the ship.

"For transporting Negroes, a fine of $5,000 and forfeiture of the ship and Negroes.

"For transporting and selling Negroes, a fine of $1,000 to $10,000, imprisonment from 5 to 10 years, and forfeiture of the ship and Negroes.

"For knowingly buying illegally imported Negroes, a fine of $800 for each Negro, and forfeiture." [4]

The third question debated was: "How shall the Interstate Coastwide Slave-Trade be protected?" After a long debate in which Mr. Randolph predicted an eventual division between the slave and free states, the bill was referred to a conference committee which finally arranged a compromise which prohibited coastal trade for the purposes of selling Negroes in ships of under forty tons.[5]

President Jefferson finally signed the act on March 2, 1807. It was entitled the "Act to prohibit the importation of slaves into any port or place within the jurisdiction of the United States, from and after the first day of January, in the year of our Lord one thousand eight hundred and eight."[6]

This was the official, if not the actual ending of the slave trade and it was due in no little measure to Jefferson's effort. The strength of the Southern States was evident during most of the debates, where Southerners such as Williams, Early and Randolph usually out-maneuvered the strong anti-slavery men such as Sloan and Bidwell. The surprising thing about the act of 1807 is the difficulty with which it was passed, even with the moral backing of the fathers of the Revolution and the strong anti-slavery party. The victory lacked the expected glory.

There were strong economic influences at work which brought slave labor into great demand in the South. Since the invention of the steam engine by Watt, England had developed a tremendous capacity in the spinning and weaving industries. Nearly all of the Southern States were given over to raising cotton for the English mills. The invention of the cotton gin in 1793, by Eli Whitney, made it possible for the southern plantation owner to separate the fibre from the seed and export a great deal more than he had previously been able to do. The South was becoming rich raising cotton and as this crop must be hand-picked, a great demand for slave labor was growing at the very time it was becoming illegal to bring them in. The institution of slavery became suddenly, something which every Southerner was anxious to defend. Moral sanctions were hastily sought in the literatures of Greece and Rome and a marked difference began to appear within the Union between the Southern and Northern States. Thus began the race between the North and South to keep the balance of newly created states equal so that one would not get the better of the other in the Senate. Thus when Indiana was admitted as a free state, in 1816, it was balanced by the slave state Mississippi in 1817. In 1818 Illinois was admitted as a free state; a year later Alabama, as a slave state, kept the score even.

All went well until the race reached the Mississippi River and came into the great territory which Jefferson had purchased from France in 1803. The question now was whether this territory should allow slavery or not. It was in 1820 that this question was settled by the so-called Missouri Compromise. The obstinacy with which the South fought for the right of making the new state of Missouri a slave state, came as a surprise to the North. The matter was finally settled by allowing Missouri to have slaves on condition that all the states which should be formed West of it and North of 36° 30' North Lat. (the line of the Southern boundary of Missouri), should be free states. Jefferson, who was then an old man and long out of office, saw clearly that the Missouri question was a grave danger to the Union. Before the Compromise had been reached he wrote, "From the Battle of Bunker Hill to the Treaty of Paris, we never had so ominous a question. . . . I thank God that I shall not live to witness its issue."[7]

At the time of the Missouri Compromise, slavery had become a political rather than a humanitarian question. The very existence of the Union was endangered because of the division which was evolving within the nation. The following excerpt from a letter dated January 22, 1821, shows Jefferson's almost uncanny ability to foresee future events. In referring to the "Missouri question" he says:

"The real question, as seen in the States afflicted with this unfortunate population (slaves), is, are our slaves to be presented with freedom and a dagger? For if Congress has the power to regulate the conditions of the inhabitants of the States, within the States, it will be but another exercise of that power to declare that all shall be free. Are we then to see again Athenian and Lacedemonian confederacies? To wage another Peloponnesian War to settle the ascendency between them? Or is this the tocsin of merely a servile war? That remains to be seen; but not, I hope, by you or me."[8]

## Jefferson's Will and Summary of His Views

Jefferson in his will distributed the majority of his slaves to his heirs together with his property. He couldn't see his way clear to free them all. He made provision for freeing five of the most faithful of them in a codicil which was added to the original document a day later, i.e., on March 17, 1826.

"I give to my good, affectionate, and faithful servant Burwell, his freedom, and the sum of three hundred dollars, to buy necessities to commence his trade of glazier, or to use otherwise as he pleases.

"I give also to my good servants, John Hennings and Joe Fosset, their freedom at the end of one year after my death, and to each of them respectively, all the tools of their respective shops or callings; and it is my will that a comfortable log-house be built for each of the three servants so emancipated, on some part of my lands convenient to them with respect to the residence of their wives, and to Charlottesville and the University, where they will be mostly employed, and reasonably convenient also to the interests of the proprietor of the lands, of which houses I give the use of one, with a curtilage of an acre to each, during his life of personal occupation thereof.

"I also give to John Hemings the service of his two apprentices, Madison and Eston Hemings, until their respective ages of twenty-one years, at which period respectively, I give them their freedom; and I humbly and earnestly request of the legislature of Virginia a confirmation of the bequest of freedom to these servants, with permission to remain in this state, where their families and connections are, as an additional instance of the favor, of which I have received so many other manifestations in the course of my life, and for which I now give them my last, solemn, and dutiful thanks." [1]

Jefferson was born into a slaveholding family in a colony where the institution was looked upon as being both proper and necessary. From his father and the frontier environment he acquired liberal and equalitarian ideas which were unknown among the lowland planters of Eastern Virginia. In his education he was fortunate in having liberal-minded teachers, one of whom we know was strongly opposed to slavery. His mastery of Greek, Latin and Anglo Saxon was of great use to him in his legal studies, as was his ability to read French fluently, in acquainting him with the political philosophy of the times.

It can truthfully be said that none of the later abolitionists who lived between Jefferson's time and the outbreak of the Civil War in 1861, ever did more than he toward the cause of freeing the slaves. He had many times proposed legislation for the freeing and bettering of the condition of these unfortunate people and had given much thought during his life to the question of how this could be accomplished without the danger of racial mixture with the white population.

Like Washington, he had hoped that "this abominable crime" could in some way be ended by legal measures, although he never thought out the details as to how this could best be accomplished. He believed that the slaves should be sent out of the country and declared "a free and independent people." He wanted "a total emancipation . . . with the consent of the masters," for he realized that the evil of slavery was not only bad for the Negro, but also "bad for the morals of the (white) people."

Although he advanced the "suspicion" that the blacks "are inferior to the whites in the endowment both of body and mind," he was careful to point out that "whatever be their degree of talent, it is no measure of their *rights*." He was a friend "to the rights of human nature" be they black or white; for he had "sworn upon the altar of God eternal hostility against every form of tyranny over the mind of man." That is, perhaps, why he could so truthfully write the following words during the last few days he spent in the White House in 1809, "You know that nobody wishes more ardently to see an abolition, not only of the slave trade, but of the condition of slavery; and certainly, nobody will be more willing to encounter every sacrifice for that object."

# PART V.

# James Madison's
# Views on Negro Slavery

## I.

### The Importance of Madison's Views

James Madison was born on March 16, 1751, at Port Conway, King George County, Virginia. His father, also named James, owned large estates worked by slaves in Orange County, Virginia. The boy was brought up in much the same environment and circumstances as both Washington and Jefferson. The family was an old one, at least according to American estimation. The first ancestor was thought to have been the Captain Isaac Maddyson mentioned by Captain John Smith as being in the colony as early as 1623. Enjoying the advantages of wealth and social prominence, young Madison was sent to the College of New Jersey, now Princeton University, in 1769, where he was graduated in 1771. After studying theology a year, he returned to Virginia where he continued his reading of Hebrew and theology while acting as a tutor for the younger members of his family.

With the outbreak of the Revolutionary War, his theological ambitions gave way to political ones. His first public post was chairman of the committee of public safety for Orange County in 1775. In the spring of 1776 he was elected to represent Orange County in the Virginia convention. There, he was chosen one of the committee which drafted the constitution of that state. In 1779 he was elected a delegate to the Continental Congress where his ability as a legislator became recognized. It was he who, when an import duty was debated which should be paid by all the states, first suggested that this should be done by distributing the burden among the states according to their population, with the slaves counting as three-fifths of the white population. In fact it was Madison who first suggested this ratio which afterwards formed the compromise between the Northern and Southern States in the Constitutional Convention.

When his term of office expired in 1783, he returned to Virginia and began the study of law but returned one year later to the Virginia House of Delegates. It was here on December 26, 1785 that he introduced Jefferson's bill for establishing religious freedom. It was he who drew up the so called "Virginia plan," which formed the basis of the United States Constitution which was voted upon by the Convention on Sept. 17, 1787. From the very first, an opponent of slavery, he fought the postponement of the prohibition of the slave trade until the year 1808.

Madison's role in the Convention which wrote the United States Constitution can hardly be overestimated. Some claim that he was in reality the father of that document. All his life, he was considered as an expert on constitutional law and was often consulted when questions arose. He served as Secretary of State under Jefferson and was twice elected President of the United States (1810–1817). Upon retiring from that office he settled down at his country estate, Montpelier, which was modeled after Jefferson's Monticello, and which like the latter, nearly ruined its owner financially. During these years (1817 until his death in 1836) he rested somewhat on his fame, keeping up a large correspondence with the prominent men of his time. It was then that he first really gave much thought to the plight of the slaves.

At the time of the "Missouri question" (1819–1820) he was consulted by President Monroe, his follower, on constitutional problems brought up by the issue, and in February, 1833, at the advanced age of eighty-two accepted the office of president of the American Colonization Society.

The first mention having to do with Madison's views on slavery to be found among his published letters, is a short note addressed to his friend, Edmond Randolph, and dated July 26, 1785. In it he says, "My wish is, if possible, to provide a decent and independent subsistence without encountering the difficulties which I forsee in that line. Another of my wishes is to depend as little as possible upon the labor of slaves." [1] He was thirty-four years old when this was written and was an active member of the Virginia House of Delegates which was then occupied with Thomas Jefferson's reforms. During his whole life he was greatly influenced by Jefferson whom he loved like a brother.

Writing to Jefferson, who was then representing the United States in France, to keep him informed as to the progress of the Virginia legislature, Madison says, "several petitions (from Methodists, chiefly) appeared in favor of a gradual abolition of slavery, and several from another quarter for a repeal of the law which licenses manumissions. The former were not thrown under the table but were treated with all the indignity short of it. A proposition for bringing in a bill conformably to the latter was decided in the affirmative by the casting voice of the speaker; but the bill was thrown out on the first reading by a considerable majority." [2]

## II.

### Madison at the Federal Convention of 1787

Madison was one of the delegates from Virginia who took part in the famous Federal Convention of 1787 in which the present Constitution of the United States was framed. The convention lasted four months and was presided over by General Washington.

The main purpose of the Convention was to get the American people represented in a body which could rightfully tax the whole people. Most of the delegates were afraid to broach the problems having to do with slavery because they believed it was one which, if left alone, would gradually adjust itself. A general silence on the subject of slavery and the slave trade was therefore maintained at first, but this soon broke out into a violent debate in which the ethics of the institution played a prominent part. But, the first stand taken by the delegates from Georgia and South Carolina could not be overcome. After the first outburst began to die down, a "middle ground" was sought to bring about a general agreement. Consequently a "bargain" was made, which like most bargains, merely prolonged the issue into the future instead of courageously facing the facts. The bargain was first proposed by General Pinckney who suggested the extension of the slave-trading limit until the year 1808—a period of some twenty years. To this proposal, Madison vigorously protested, saying: "Twenty years will produce all the mischief that can be apprehended from the liberty to import slaves. So long a term will be more dishonorable to the American character than to say nothing about it in the constitution."[1] In a later debate, Madison fought any recognition of property in man, i.e., taxable property.[2] Washington remained silent, losing the opportunity of throwing the weight of his prestige against slavery.

The "bargain" that was finally made was written into the Constitution under Article I, Section 9. It reads as follows: "The Migration or Importation of such Persons as any of the States now existing shall think proper to admit, shall not be prohibited by the Congress prior to the Year one thousand eight hundred and eight, but a Tax or Duty may be imposed on such Importation, not exceeding ten dollars for each Person." It is well to note how cleverly this article pertaining to the slaves was worded so that the hated word "slave" would not appear. Madison explains just why this came about, in a letter written to General Lafayette some forty-three years later: ". . . I scarcely express myself too strongly in saying, that any illusion in the Convention to the subject you have so much at heart (the freeing of the slaves) would have been a spark to a mass of gunpowder."[3] In another letter he says that "Some of the states . . . had scruples against admitting the term 'slaves' into the instrument. Hence the descriptive phrase, 'migration or importation of persons' . . . allowing those who were scrupulous of acknowledging expressly a property in human beings to view *imported* persons as a species of immigrants. . . . It is possible . . . that some might have had an eye to the case of freed blacks as well. . . ."[4]

Thus was the shameful "bargain" made and the twenty-one year period of "laissez-faire" entered into which Madison had denounced as "dishonorable to

the American character." The Union had been preserved but the real decision had only begun its long
career of postponement. In the note-book which Madison kept during the convention, the following sentence appears: "Where slavery exists, the republican
theory becomes still more fallacious." [5]

Four months later[6] Madison wrote the following
paragraph in an article which appeared unsigned in
the New York "Packet":

"It were doubtless to be wished, that the power of
prohibiting the importation of slaves had not been
postponed until the year 1808, or rather that it had
been suffered to have immediate operation. But it is
not difficult to account, either for this restriction on
the general government, or for the manner in which
the whole clause is expressed. It ought to be considered
as a great point gained in favor of humanity, that a
period of twenty years may terminate forever, within
these states, a traffic which has so long and so loudly
upbraided the barbarism of modern policy; that within that period, it will receive a considerable discour-
agement from the federal government, and may be
totally abolished, by a concurrence of the few states
which continue the unnatural traffic, in the prohibitory example which has been given by so great a
majority of the Union. Happy would it be for the
unfortunate Africans, if an equal prospect lay before
them of being redeemed from the oppressions of their
European brethren!" [7]

When an old man of eighty years, Madison was
still sensitive to the inconsistency of slavery and the
principles set forth in the Declaration of Independence. He attempted to defend the "status quo" by
claiming that the position of the United States

". . . rests on a foundation too just and solid to be shaken by any technical or metaphysical arguments whatever. The known and acknowledged intentions of the parties at the time (that the Constitution was agreed upon), with a perspective sanction of so many years consecrated by the intrinsic principles of equity, would overrule even the most explicit declarations and terms (such as expressed in the Declaration of Independence) as has been done without the aid of that principle in the slaves, who remain such in spite of the declarations that all men are born equally free."[8]

In the fall of 1791, a Mr. Robert Pleasants wrote to Madison urging him to present a petition to Congress requesting that the slaves be freed. This was one of the many petitions and memorials which flooded Congress, the first being that of the Quakers and that of the Pennsylvania Abolition Society of which Franklin was president. Madison wrote to Mr. Pleasants from Philadelphia on October 30, 1791. Knowing the futility of such attempts owing to the stand which the representatives from the states of South Carolina and Georgia had taken, Madison very diplomatically refused to present the petition. Speaking of the slaves, he reminded Mr. Pleasants that "Those from whom I derive my public station are known by me to be greatly interested in that species of property. . . . It would seem that I might be chargeable at least with want of candour, if not fidelity were I . . . to become a volunteer in giving a public wound, as they would deem it, to an interest on which they set so great a value."

Madison was not, as we shall see later, in favor of setting the slaves free without some provision having been made for their removal. Accordingly he adds,

"It may be worth your own consideration whether it might not produce successful attempts to withdraw the privilege now allowed to individuals, of giving freedom to slaves. It would at least be likely to clog it with a condition that the persons freed should be removed from the country; there being arguments of great force for such a regulation, and some would concur in it, who, in general, disapprove of the institution of slavery." [9]

## III.

### As President of the United States

There is a curious gap in Madison's letters in which no mention of the slave-trade or slavery is to be found for a period of nearly twenty years. And yet this can be explained on the ground that no slave problem existed. The Constitution had made the slave trade legal in three states [1] and the rest of the nation were patiently waiting until 1808 to do away with it altogether. During President Jefferson's second term of office the famous Act of 1807 was passed which made the slave trade illegal, but when Madison followed his friend in that office in 1809, he found that the mere passage of an act had not really put an end to the practice. Accordingly, in his message to Congress in December, 1810, he said that . . .

"Among the commercial abuses still under the American flag . . . it appears that American citizens are instrumental in carrying on a traffic in enslaved Africans, equally in violation of the laws of humanity, and in defiance of those of their own country. The same just and benevolent motives which produced the interdiction in force against this criminal conduct, will doubtless be felt by Congress, in devising further means of suppressing the evil." [2]

In his address to the Fourteenth Congress, delivered on December 3, 1816, President Madison said:

"The United States having been the first to abolish, within the extent of their authority, the transportation of the natives of Africa into slavery, by prohibiting the introduction of slaves, and by punishing their citizens participating in the traffic, cannot but be gratified at the progress, made by concurrent efforts of other nations, toward a general suppression of so great an evil. They must feel, at the same time, the greater solicitude to give the fullest efficacy to their own regulations. With that view, the interposition of Congress appears to be required by the violations and evasions which, it is suggested, are chargeable on unworthy citizens, who mingle in the slave trade under foreign flags, and with foreign ports; and by collusive importations of slaves into the United States, through adjoining ports and territories. I present the subject to Congress, with a full assurance of their disposition to apply all the remedy which can be afforded by an amendment of the law. The regulations which are intended to guard against abuses of a kindred character, in the trade between the several states, ought also to be rendered more effectual for their humane object." [3]

Madison did all that he could to check these abuses of the law, but the tide had turned and the slave power was too well established for him to succeed.

## IV.

### Madison's Plan For Emancipation

It was not until the year 1819, when Madison had retired to his Montpelier estate in Virginia, that he actually worked out his plan as to how emancipation could best be brought about. It is evident to anyone who is acquainted with Jefferson's ideas on this subject, that Madison was greatly influenced by his friend. On the other hand, Madison thought out many of the practical difficulties which Jefferson failed to visualize. Henry Clay, contrasting Madison with Jefferson, said that Jefferson had more genius, Madison more judgment and commonsense; that Jefferson was a visionary and a theorist; that Madison was cool, dispassionate, practical and safe.[1]

Madison says that emancipation should be gradual, equitable and satisfactory to all the persons concerned. "That it ought, like remedies for other deep-rooted and widespread evils, to be gradual, is so obvious, that there seems to be no difference of opinion on that point. To be equitable and satisfactory, the consent of both the master and slave should be obtained.[2]

"To be consistent with existing and probably unalterable prejudices in the United States, the freed blacks ought to be permanently removed beyond the region occupied by, or allotted to, a white population. The objections to a thorough incorporation of the two people are . . . insuperable."[3] It is necessary, then, to remove the blacks far enough away that they will not come into contact with "a neighboring people, stimulated by a contempt known to be entertained for their peculiar features." In all fairness he reminds us that we cannot ". . . charge it wholly on the side of the blacks . . ." and that these are ". . . reciprocal antipathies doubling the danger." [4]

At this point we might ask why it was that the Colonization Society could not accomplish the emancipation? But Madison recognized that this society was only concerned with transporting "free or freed blacks" to Africa and was not concerned with freeing the slaves at all. So he suggests that the experiment merits encouragement from all who regard slavery as an evil and who have themselves no better mode to propose and that those who have most doubted the success of the experiment must, at least, have wished to find themselves in an error.[5]

He was not satisfied with the Colonization Society because it was "limited to the case of blacks already free, or who may be *gratuitously* emancipated." The plan must be extended to "the great mass of blacks, and must embrace a fund sufficient to induce the master, as well as the slave, to concur in it." [6] For why should the patriotic and philanthropic masters be asked to bear so great a burden in the loss of valuable property?

He thought that it would be unfair to expect voluntary contributions from the masters to bring about this end. "It is the nation which is to reap the benefit. The nation therefore ought to bear the burden." [7]

"It is a peculiar fortune . . . of the United States to possess a resource commensurate to this great object, without taxes on the people, or even an increase of public debt. I allude to the vacant territory, the extent of which is so vast. . . ." [8] Herein lies Madison's solution of the problem. It was not to Africa, but the vacant territory in the West that the Negroes should be sent. This idea never occurred to Jefferson. In fact Jefferson never troubled himself much with the problem from a practical standpoint. Madison was, himself, not too optimistic about his own plan, for only one year later he wrote: "I have long thought that our vacant territory was the resource which, in some mode or other, was most applicable and adequate without, however, being unaware that even that would as a general cure for the portentous evil (slaves); encounter serious difficulties of different sorts." [9]

He then examines the cost of this scheme to the United States which he estimates at six hundred million dollars, "supposing the numbers of slaves to be 1,500,000, and their price to average 400 dollars...." Deduction must be made for those "gratuitously" set free, those set free by state regulations, those who do not want to risk removal and would rather remain slaves, and those "slaves whom their masters would not part with." Although these instances would reduce the cost considerably ". . . on the other hand, it is to be noted that the expense of removal and settlement is not included in the estimated sum; and that the increase of slaves will be going on during the period required for the execution of the plan."

He thought that an extra 300 million dollars would be necessary for the purchase of 200 million acres of land at three dollars an acre ". . . perhaps not a third part of the disposable territory belonging to the United States. And to what object so good, so great, and so glorious, could that peculiar fund of wealth be appropriated?" He added that ". . . if in any instances wrong has been done by our forefathers to people of one color, by dispossessing them of their soil, what better atonement is now in our power than making what is rightfully acquired a source of justice and of blessings to a people of another color?" In other words, because the whites robbed the Indians of their land, the whites can now make atonement by giving it to the Negroes!

But the plan must proceed slowly.

"Masters would not be willing to strip their plantations and farms of their laborers too rapidly. The slaves themselves, connected, as they generally are, by tender ties under other masters, would be kept from the list of emigrants by the want of the multiplied consents to be obtained."

He points out that the states which have a common interest in the vacant territory but have no interest in slave property are "... too just to wish that a partial sacrifice should be made for the general good, and too well aware that whatever may be the intrinsic character of that description of property, it is one known to the Constitution, and, as such, could not be constitutionally taken away without just compensation."

Madison is conscious that, in the carrying out of his plan, difficulties of all sorts would be encountered. Among these difficulties he mentions those of reasonable valuations, which would require the mature deliberations of the national councils.

As the best legislative provision, he advises the incorporation of the Colonization Society, or the establishment of a similar one under the appointment and superintendence of the National Executive.

He ends by advising that any plan for freeing the slaves "ought to be brought into comparison with ... other plans, and be yielded to or not according to the result of the comparison." "... Whatever may be the defect of the existing powers of Congress, the Constitution has pointed out the way in which it (this defect) can be supplied. And it can hardly be doubted that the requisite powers might readily be procured for attaining of the great object in question, in any mode whatever approved by the nation."

## V.

### Letters Further Illustrating His Plan

Writing to General Lafayette in 1821, Madison gives us a splendid summary of the status of the slaves and what was being done to relieve them at this time.

"The Negro slavery is, as you justly complain, a sad blot on our free country, though a very ungracious subject of reproaches from the quarter (England) which has been most lavish of them. No satisfactory plan has yet been devised for taking out the stain. If an asylum could be found in Africa, that would be the appropriate destination for the unhappy race among us. Some are sanguine that the efforts of an existing Colonization Society will accomplish such a provision: but a very partial success seems the most that can be expected. Some other region must therefore, be found for them as they become free and willing to emigrate. The repugnance of the whites to their continuance among them is founded on prejudices, themselves founded upon physical distinctions, which are not likely soon, if ever, to be eradicated. Even in States, Massachusetts for example, which displayed most sympathy with the people of color on the Missouri question, prohibitions are taking place against their becoming residents. They are everywhere regarded as a nuisance, and must really be such as long as they are under the degradation which public sentiment inflicts on them. They are at the same time rapidly increasing from manumissions and from offsprings, and of course lessening the general disproportion between the slaves and the whites. This tendency is favorable to the cause of a universal emancipation."[1]

On September 1, 1825, Madison wrote a letter to a Miss Frances Wright, who had sent Mrs. Madison a copy of her plan for the gradual abolition of slavery in the United States, in which letter Madison pointed out that the task of devising a satisfactory remedy for this evil is made harder by the "physical peculiarities" of the slaves "which preclude their incorporation with the white population; and by the blank in the general field of labor to be occasioned by their exile. . . ." He thought that there would not be enough influx of white laborers to fill the need which would prove "distressing" for the farmers.

Continuing in his criticism of her plan, he first agrees with her as to the necessity of a "voluntary concurrence" between master and slave, and also as to the advisability of carrying on her experiment in a part of the country where there are no slaves.

Miss Wright's plan was that a great number of slaves should settle on a distant plantation where they would earn enough money not only to pay for the operation of the farm, but to buy their freedom from their masters. While they were thus working they should also receive enough education to fit them for their coming freedom.

Madison pointed out that whereas it is a fact that, where labor is compulsory, the greater the number of laborers brought together, the less are the proportional profits, it may be doubted whether the surplus from merely that source, would sufficiently accumulate in five, or even more years, for the objects in view. He adds he is not satisfied that the prospect of emancipation at a future day will be reward enough to overcome a natural and habitual repugnance to labor. Nor is he sure that there is such an advantage of united, over individual, labor as is taken for granted. The fact that the individual laborer must share his efforts with those who are not so industrial, would prove, Madison thought, a drawback rather than an incentive. He points out that where these "united labors of many for common object" have been succesful, as in the case of the Moravians, Harmonites and Shakers, there has always been "a religious impulse in the members, and a religious authority in the head, for which there will be no substitutes of equivalent efficacy in the emancipating establishment." He is doubtful whether the experiment should not be commenced better on a scale smaller than that assumed in the prospectus where " . . . the direction of their labor would be more simple and manageable." In spite of these doubts as to her plan, he admits an admiration of the generous philanthropy which created it.[2]

In a letter to General Lafayette written at Montpelier and dated merely "November, 1826," Madison makes mention again of Miss Wright's experiment. He says in part, "we learn only that she has chosen for it (her experiment) a remote spot in the western part of Tennessee, and has commenced her enterprise; but with what prospects we know not. Her plan contemplated a provision for the expatriation of her Elèves, but without specifying it; from which I infer the difficulty felt in devising a satisfactory one. Manumissions now more than keep pace with the outlets provided, and the increase of them is checked only by their remaining in the country. This obstacle removed, and all others would yield to the emancipating disposition . . . what would be more simple, with the requisite grant of power to Congress, than to purchase all the female infants at their birth, leaving them in the service of the holder to a reasonable age, on condition of their receiving an elementary education? The annual number of female births may be stated at twenty thousand, and the cost at less than one hundred dollars each, at the most; a sum that would not be felt by the nation, and be even within the compass of state resources. But no such effort would be listened to, whilst the impression remains, and it seems to be indelible, that the two races cannot co-exist, both being free and equal. The great *sine qua non*, therefore, is some external asylum for the colored race. In the meantime, the taunts to which this misfortune exposes us in Europe are the more to be deplored, because it impairs the influence of our political example, though they come out with an ill grace from the quarter most lavish of them (England), the quarter which obtruded the evil, and which has but lately become a penitent under suspicious appearances." [3]

During the years 1831 and 1832, a great debate raged in the Virginia legislature on the abolition of slavery. A review of this debate was published by Thomas R. Dew, a professor in William and Mary College, Virginia.[4] In this review, Prof. Dew took an almost violent pro-slavery position in which he defended the institution by quoting liberally not only from history, but from the New Testament. He made use of all the arguments and the logic in his power to show that removing the slaves was as impractical as setting them free was undesirable.

In the reply which Madison made to Prof. Dew after a reading of two of his pamphlets,[5] we have one of the best of Madison's expressions of his view regarding slavery.[6] After a very polite introduction, Madison tells the Professor, "in not a few of the data from which you reason, and in the conclusion to which you are led, I cannot concur."

He recognized "the impracticability of an immediate or early execution of any plan that combines deportation with emancipation and of the inadmissibility of emancipation without deportation." But he believed in the "expediency of attempting a *gradual* remedy."

"If emancipation was the sole object, the extinguishment of slavery would be easy, cheap, and complete." This could be accomplished by the public purchase of all female children, at their birth, leaving them in bondage, till it would defray the charge of rearing them.

Madison then points out that the real problem is not one of the expense involved actually in emancipating and exporting the slaves but "in the attainment: 1, of the requisite asylums; 2, the consent of the individuals to be removed; 3, the labor for the vacuum to be created."

He is of the opinion that the expense can be cut down by voluntary emancipations, increasing under the influence of example, and that much might be expected in gifts and legacies from the opulent and the conscientious; still more from legislative grants by the states and aid from the indirect or direct proceeds of the public lands held in trust by Congress.

Nor is Madison so discouraged over the difficulty of attaining adequate asylums for the slaves. ". . . Africa, though the primary, is not the sole asylum within contemplation." He suggests "the islands adjoining this continent (West Indies) where the colored population is already dominent, and where the wheel of revolution may from time to time produce the like result." Nor should the territory under the control of the United States be overlooked, because it is sufficiently distant to avoid, for an indefinite period, the collisions to be apprehended from the vicinity of people distinguished from each other by physical as well as other characteristics.

Another of the problems involved in the emancipation of the slaves was to get the consent of the individuals themselves to be removed. Madison reminds Prof. Dew that among the free blacks there is a known repugnance . . . to leave their native homes, while among the slaves, there is an almost universal preference of their present condition to freedom in a distant and unknown land. He is of the opinion that the prejudices arise from a distrust of the favorable accounts coming to them through white channels. But "by degrees the truth will find its way."

The third problem in connection with deportation is the difficulty of filling the vacancies left by the slaves with other laborers. His answer is that first, the remaining whites will increase and secondly, there will be an attraction of whites from without. Thirdly, "as the culture of tobacco declines," on account of "the successful competition in the West, and as the farming system takes the place of the planting, a portion of labor can be spared without impairing the requisite stock." Madison freely admits that "the process must be slow, be attended with much inconvenience, and be not even certain in its result." ". . . Is it not preferable," he asks, "to a torpid acquiescence in a perpetuation of slavery, or an extinguishment of it by convulsions more disastrous in their character and consequences than slavery itself?" [7]

## VI.

### The "Queries" and Some Statistics

On March 14, 1823, a Dr. Morse, sent the following list of "Queries" from "a respectable correspondent in Liverpool, deeply engaged in the abolition of the slave trade, and the amelioration of the condition of slaves." Dr. Morse begged Madison to answer these questions "briefly to serve the cause of humanity, and gratify and oblige the society above named." [1] I give the questions and answers which seem to throw the most light on the actual condition of the slaves and Madison's views.

1. Do the planters generally live on their own estates?
Answer: Yes.

2. Does a planter with ten or fifteen slaves employ an overlooker, or does he overlook his slaves himself?
Answer: Employs an overlooker for the number of slaves with few exceptions.

4. Is it a common or general practice to mortgage slave estates?
Answer: Not uncommonly the land; sometimes the slaves; very rarely both.

5. Are the sales of slave estates very frequent under execution for debt, and what proportion of the whole may thus be sold annually?
Answer: The common law, as in England, governs the relation between land and debts; slaves are often sold under execution for debt, the proportion to the whole cannot be great within a year, and varies of course, with the amount of debts and the urgency of creditors.

6. Does the Planter possess the power of selling the different branches of a family separate?
Answer: Yes.

7. When the prices of produce, cotton, sugar, etc., are high, do the Planters purchase, instead of raising their corn and other provisions?

8. When the prices of produce are low, do they then raise their own corn and other provisions?

9. Do the Negroes fare better when the corn, etc., is raised upon their master's estate or when he buys it?

10. Do the tobacco planters in America ever buy their own corn or other food, or do they always raise it?

Answers to questions 7, 8, 9, and 10: Instances are rare where the tobacco planters do not raise their own provisions.

17. Are there many small plantations where the owners possess only a few slaves? What proportion of the whole may be supposed to be held in this way?
Answer: Very many, and increasing with the progressive subdivisions of property; the proportions cannot be stated.

18. In such cases, are the slaves treated or almost considered a part of the family?

19. Do the slaves fare the best when their situations and that of the masters are brought nearest together?
Answer to questions 18 and 19: The fewer the slaves, and the fewer the holders of slaves, the greater the indulgence and familiarity. In districts composing (comprising?) large masses of slaves there is no difference in their condition, whether held in small or large numbers, beyond the difference in the disposi-

tions of the owners, and the greater strictness of attention where the number is greater.

20. In what state are the slaves as to religion or religious instruction?

Answer: There is no general system of religious instruction. There are few spots where religious worship is not within reach, and to which they do not resort. Many are regular members of congregations, chiefly Baptist; and some Preachers also, though rarely able to read.

21. Is it common for slaves to be regularly married?

Answer: Not common; but the instances are increasing.

22. If a man forms an attachment to a woman on a different or distant plantation, is it the general practice for some accommodation to take place between the owners of the man and the woman, so that they may live together?

Answer: The accommodation not unfrequent where the plantations are very distant. The slaves prefer wives on a distant plantation, as affording occasions and pretexts for going abroad, and exempting them on holidays from a share of the little calls to which those at home are liable.

26. Is it common for free blacks to labor in the field?

Answer: They are sometimes hired for field labor in time of harvest, and on other particular occasions.

29. Is it considered that the increase in the proportion of free blacks to slaves increases or diminishes the danger of insurrection?

Answer: Rather increases.

31. Do the free blacks appear to consider themselves as more closely connected with the slaves or with

the white population? And in cases of insurrection, with which have they generally taken part?

Answer: More closely with the slaves, and more likely to side with them in a case of insurrection.

32. What is their general character with respect to industry and order, as compared with that of slaves?

Answer: Generally idle and depraved; appearing to retain the bad qualities of the slaves, with whom they continue to associate, without acquiring any of the good ones of the whites, from whom they continue separated by prejudices against their color, and other peculiarities.

33. Are there any instances of emancipation in particular estates, and what is the result?

Answer: There are occasional instances in the present legal condition of leaving the state.

34. Is there any general plan of emancipation in progress, and what?

Answer: None.

Madison closes the letter, with which he returned these answers to Dr. Morse, with a regret that "the answers could not conveniently be extended as much as might, perhaps, be desired."

In another letter, he contrasts the condition of the slaves then (1819) and before the Revolution. In Virginia, he finds it "better, beyond comparison . . . better fed, better clad, better lodged, and better treated in every respect." He gives two main reasons for this:

"1. The sensibility to human rights and sympathy with human sufferings" issuing from "the spirit of the Institutions growing out of, that event." (The Revolution.)

"2. The decreasing proportion which the slaves bear to the individual holders of them. . . ."

He then points out that the general condition of the slaves is dependent upon the following factors:

"1.   The ordinary price of food, on which the quality and quantity allowed them will more or less depend."

"2.   The kind of labor to be performed." He mentions sugar and rice plantations as unfavorable examples.

"3.   The national spirit of their masters, which has been graduated by philosophic writers among the slave-holding Colonies of Europe."

"4.   The circumstances of conformity or difference in physical character," i.e. color, features, etc. The whiter slaves are often better treated than the darker ones.

"5.   The proportion which the slaves bear to the free part of the community, and especially the greater or smaller numbers in which they belong to individuals," [2]

On April 21, 1821, he wrote to Mr. Rush deploring the falsification of statistics regarding the black population of the United States.

"Between the years 1790 and 1810 the number of slaves increased from 694,280 to 1,165,441. This increase, at a rate nearly equal to that of the whites, surely was not produced by emigrants from Africa. Nor could any part of it have been imported (except 30 or 40,000 into South Carolina and Georgia), the prohibition being everywhere strictly enforced throughout that period. Louisiana, indeed, brought an addition amounting in 1810 to 37,671. This number, however (to be reduced by the slaves carried thither from other states prior to 1810), may be regarded as overbalanced by emancipated blacks and their subsequent offspring. The whole number of this description in the census of 1810 amounts to 186,446."

"The evidence of a natural and rapid increase of the blacks in the State of Virginia is alone conclusive on the subject. Since the epoch of Independence the importation of slaves has been uniformly prohibited, and the spirit of the people concurring with the policy of the law, it has been carried fully into execution. Yet the number of slaves increased from 292,627 in 1790, to 372,518 in 1810; although it is notorious that very many have been carried from the state by external purchases and migrating masters. In the state of Maryland, to the north of Virginia, whence alone it could be surmised that any part of them could be replaced, there has been also an increase."

## VII.

### The Constitution and the Missouri Question

When Madison left the presidency of the United States in 1817, he retired to his estate "Montpelier" where he was consulted on all the important problems of his day and where he had the time to carry on a large correspondence with the nation's leaders. As one of the few living men who had taken an active part in the framing of the American Constitution, his advice on matters pertaining to it was of particular value, and that is why, when the vexing problem in connection with the newly admitted state of Missouri arose, his opinion was so eagerly sought.

We are not concerned here with the Missouri question, as such, but rather, with Madison's opinions, which throw light upon his attitude toward the institution of Negro slavery.

While the Missouri question was still in debate, a Mr. Robert Walsh wrote to Madison asking his opinion as to the meaning of the framers of the Constitution in the clause referring to "the migration and importation of persons." He wanted to know if the framers had in mind the immigration and importation of Negroes from outside the United States or whether the clause implied that Negroes could not move about within the limits of the United States itself. Madison's reply, dated November 27, 1819 at his home Montpelier, says in part:

"As to the intention of the framers of the Constitution . . . the best key may, perhaps, be found in the case which produced it."

After reviewing the history of the case, he relates:

"But, whatever may have been intended by the term 'migration,' or the term 'persons' it is most certain that they referred exclusively to amigration or importation from other countries into the United States, and not a removal, voluntary, of slaves or freemen from one to another part of the United States."

He then adds that "the great object of the Convention seemed to be to prohibit the increase by the *importation of slaves*."

"On the whole the Missouri question, as a constitutional one, amounts to the question whether the condition proposed to be annexed to the admission of Missouri would or would not be void in itself, or become void the moment the territory should enter as a state within the pale of the Constitution. And as a question of expediency and humanity, it depends essentially on the probable influence of such restrictions on the quantity and duration of slavery, and on the general condition of slaves in the United States."

With an anxious and prophetic eye to the future, the aged statesman ends his letter:

". . . the tendency of what has passed and is passing fills me with no slight anxiety. . . . Should a state of parties founded on geographical boundaries . . . what is to control those great repulsive masses from awful shocks against each other?" [1]

In a letter to President Monroe, February 10, 1820, Madison finds that

". . . the idea is fast spreading that the zeal with which the extension, so called, of slavery is opposed, has, with the coalesced *leaders*, an object very different from the welfare of the slaves, or the check of their increase; and that their real object is, as you intimate, to form a new state of parties, founded on local instead of political distinctions, thereby dividing the Republicans of the North from those of the South, and making the former instrumental in giving to the opponents of both an ascendency over the whole."

"I have been truly astonished at some of the doctrines and deliberations to which the Missouri question has led, and particularly so as to the interpretations, put on the terms 'migration or importation, etc.' judging from my own impressions, I should deem it impossible that the memory of anyone who was a member of the General Convention, could favor an opinion that the terms did not *exclusively* refer to migration and importation *into the United States*. Had they been understood in that body in the sense now put on them, it is easy to conceive the alienation they would have then created in certain states. . . ."

"If a suspicion had existed of such a construction, it would at least have made a conspicuous figure among the amendments proposed to the instrument."

"I have observed as yet, in none of the views taken of the Ordinance of 1787, interdicting slavery N. W. of the Ohio, an allusion to the circumstance that, when if passed, the Congress had no authority to prohibit the importation of slaves from abroad; that all the states had, and some were in the full exercise of the right to import them; and consequently, that there was no mode in which Congress could check the evil but the indirect one of narrowing the space open for the reception of slaves. Had a federal authority then existed to prohibit directly and totally the importation from abroad, can it be doubted that it would have been exerted? and that a regulation having merely the effect of preventing an interior dispersion of the slaves actually in the United States, and creating a distinction among the states in the degrees of their sovereignty, would not have been adopted, or perhaps thought of?" [2]

Two weeks later Madison wrote again to President Monroe regarding the Missouri Compromise which had restricted slavery "forever" in the territory west of the Mississippi River and north of 36° 30' North latitude, this line being the southern boundary of that state. The question as to whether Congress had the right to restrict slavery in Missouri as long as it was a territory cannot be questioned.[3] The question now was whether Missouri as a state and no longer a territory came under the "rules and regulations" of Congress. Had it not the right now to restrict or confirm slavery according to the principle of self-government? Madison thought that it had. He said " . . . I must own that I have always leaned to the belief that the restriction was not within the true scope of the Constitution." He held this belief not because he wished to further slavery but because he believed that "an uncontrolled dispersion of slaves" was "best for the nation . . . and for the slaves also, both as to their prospects of emancipation and their condition in the meantime." [4]

Writing to General Lafayette, Madison gives us a very good picture of how the Missouri question stood in the year 1820 which question he attributes to "the original sin of the African trade."

He tells the General that "the subject which ruffles the surface of public affairs most, at present, is furnished by the transmission of the 'Territory' of Missouri from a state of nonage to a maturity for self-government, and for a membership in the Union. Among the questions involved in it, the one most immediately interesting to humanity is the question whether a toleration or prohibition of slavery westward of the Mississippi would most extend its evils. The humane part of the argument against the prohibition turns on the position, that whilst the importation of slaves from abroad is precluded, a diffusion of those in the country tends at once to meliorate their actual condition, and to facilitate their eventual emancipation. Unfortunately, the subject, which was settled at the last session of Congress by a mutual concession of the parties, is reproduced on the arena by a clause in the Constitution of Missouri, distinguishing between free persons of color and white persons, and providing that the Legislature of the new state shall exclude from it the former. What will be the issue of the revived discussion is yet to be seen. The case opens the wider field, as the constitutions and laws of the differ-

ent states are much at variance in the civil character
given to free persons of color; those of most of the
states, not excepting such as have abolished slavery,
imposing various disqualifications, which degrade them
from the rank and rights of white persons. All these
perplexities develop more and more the dreadful fruitfulness of the original sin of the African trade." [5]

A month later (Dec. 28, 1820) Madison wrote to
President Monroe, regarding the Missouri affair. He
remarks that it is a happy circumstance that the discussions renewed by the offensive clause introduced by
Missouri are marked by such mitigated feelings in Congress and that the spirit and manner of conducting the
opposition to the new state, with the palpable efforts
to kindle lasting animosity between geographical divi-
sions of the nation, will have a natural tendency to
unite those who never differed as to the essential principles and the true policy of the government. [6]

# VIII.

## Madison and Colonization Society

The American Colonization Society was founded in
1816 at Washington and it was not long before its
auxiliary societies spread to most of the states. In its
constitution there was no specific mention of the object
of the society other than it was "to be exclusively
directed" to colonizing the free people of color. It was
this failure to state its definite purpose which brought
many friends and enemies of slavery togther in one
organization. Henry Wilson [1] says "it was always
singularly inconsistent and illogical. It yielded . . . to
the wicked prejudice against race and color; and yet it
called upon Churches and Christians to assist in sus-

taining it. It . . . defamed the free people of color; and yet insisted they were the preordained instruments of Heaven for the civilization of Africa. It evinced the most undisguised hostility to Abolition and Abolitionists; and yet it persistently pressed its claims on the friends of the slave." He adds that "its influence was largely instrumental in producing that sad demoralization of the nation which rendered possible . . . the triumphs of the Slave Power."

At the very first meeting of this society, which was organized to colonize the free people of color, Henry Clay of Kentucky, one of the most prominent statesmen of his day and himself a slave holder, praised the society's purpose to "rid our country of a useless and pernicious, if not dangerous, portion of its population." [2] John Randolph of Virginia thought that the object of the society was that it should not interfere with slavery or try to free the slaves, but "must materially tend to secure the property of every master in the United States in his slaves." [3] Mr. Clay again declared later that, "of all classes of our population, the most vicious is that of the free colored people." [4] These were some of the reasons given why they should be sent out of the country. The idea was to ship the free Negroes back to Africa and turn them loose in the jungles, the theory being that they would spread the religion and culture of the whites among the wild natives. How they could have expected Negroes of such a degraded class as they claimed them to be, to carry on this work is one of the illogical aspects of the society. The free blacks themselves protested against it. They didn't want to be shipped away to a strange land. Their appeal to the society read in part:

"Many of our fathers and some of us have fought

and bled for the liberty, independence, and peace which you now enjoy; and surely it would be ungenerous and unfeeling in you to deny us a humble and quiet grave in that country which gave us birth." [5]

Wilson declares that the real intent and *animus* of the movement were never in the interest of freedom, and that its avowed aim was to render slavery and its supporters more secure.[6] The Northern anti-slavery members were giving money to this society thinking that it was doing a great good to Africa by returning these people to its shores, while in reality the society was "a plan of slave-holders to get rid of the free Negroes." [7] As a matter of fact only one thousand Negroes were shipped back to Africa during the first twelve years of the society's existence. William Lloyd Garrison, the famous New England abolitionist, was one of the few men to penetrate its deceptions and to openly fight and expose its evils. He claimed that its real purpose was to "rivet still closer the fetters of the slaves and to deepen the prejudice against the free people of color." [8]

It must be remembered that many of the society's members were good citizens who were themselves ignorant of its real purposes. The real blame for the deception is now known to have been the reverend clergy who were benefiting by the contributions. Such was, in brief, the early history of the American Colonization Society. It is now time to examine Madison's relation to it and his opinions of it.

We have seen that in 1819, when he first began to give serious thought to the problems connected with slavery, he recommended putting the Colonization Society under the direct supervision of the President of the United States.[9] The motive behind this sugges-

tion was that the Federal Government was best fitted
to direct the exportation of these unfortunate people.
In his plan for effecting emancipation, he was not
satisfied with the society because it was "limited to the
case of blacks already free, or who may be *gratuitously*
emancipated." The plan, he said, must extend to "the
great mass of blacks, and must embrace a fund sufficient to induce the master as well as the slave, to concur in it." [10]

Writing in November of 1820 to a Mr. F. Corbin,
who had complained of the hard times and who
wanted to sell his slaves and convert his money into
paper securities, Madison said:

"I do not mean to discuss the question how far
*slavery* and *farming* are incompatible. Our opinions
agree as to the evil, moral, political, and economical,
of the former. I still think, notwithstanding, that under all the disadvantages of slave cultivation, much
improvement in it is practicable. Proofs are annually
taking place . . . where slaves are held in small numbers, by good masters and managers. As to the very
wealthy proprietors, much less is to be said." [11]

Again in 1821 in considering the problem of where
the blacks should be sent, he sounds a pessimistic note
as to the efforts of the Colonization Society. The Society had proposed Africa as an asylum. Madison says,
"some are sanguine that the efforts of an existing
Colonization Society will accomplish such a provision:
but a very partial success seems the most that can be
expected." [12]

Nine years later (Feb. 1, 1830) at the age of seventy-
nine, in a letter to General Lafayette, Madison begins
suddenly to show more respect for the Colonizing
Society. Referring to the freeing of the slaves, a subject

that was of great interest to Lafayette, Madison says: "It is certain...that time the 'Great Innovator,' is not idle in its salutary preparations. The Colonization Society is becoming more and more one of its agents. Outlets for the freed blacks are alone wanted for a rapid erasure of the blot from our Republican character." [13]

When Madison was eighty years old, a Protestant clergyman named Gurley who was very interested in the Colonization Society affairs, wrote to him to ask his opinion of the Colonization Society and various matters in connection with it. Madison answered that " . . . the society had always my good wishes, though with hopes of its success less sanguine than others. . . ." The prospects at the present time for the success of the Society seem to show that " . . . the time will come when the dreadful calamity which has so long afflicted our country, and filled so many with despair, will be gradually removed, and by means consistent with justice, peace, and the general satisfaction; thus giving to our country the full enjoyment of the blessings of liberty, and to the world the full benefit of its great example. I have never considered the main difficulty of the great work as lying in the deficiency of emancipations, but in an inadequacy of asylums for the growing mass of population, and in the great expense of moving it (the slaves) to its new home."

Madison then remarks that while the Colonization Society's prospect in Africa seems ". . . to be expanding in a highly encouraging degree," nevertheless, "in contemplating the pecuniary resources needed for the removal of such a number (of slaves) to so great a distance, my thoughts and hopes have long been turned to the rich fund presented in western lands of the nation, which will soon entirely cease to be

under a pledge for another object." It is known, he
adds, that "... distinguished patriots not dwelling in
slave-holding states ... would be willing to let the national domain be a resource in effectuating it. ... I am
aware of the constitutional obstacle which has presented itself; but if the general will be reconciled to an
application of the territorial fund to the removal of
the colored population, a grant to Congress of the
necessary authority could be carried with little delay
through the forms of the Constitution." [14]

A year later the Rev. Gurley wrote again to Madison,
this time informing the eighty-two year old statesman
that he had been elected, without having been consulted, President of the Colonization Society.

The following is Madison's letter in reply dated at
Montpelier on February 19, 1833, accepting the
presidency of the Society:

"Dear Sir,—I have received your letter of the 12th,
informing me that I have been unanimously elected
to the office of President by the American Colonization Society.

"The great and growing importance of the society
and the signal philanthropy of its members give to the
distinction conferred on me a value of which I am
deeply sensible.

"It is incumbent on me, at the same time to say,
that my very advanced age and impared health leave
me no hope of an adequacy to the duties of the
station which I should be proud to perform. It will
not the less be my earnest prayer that every success
may reward the labors of an Institution which, though
so humble in its origin, is so noble in its object of
removing a great evil from its own country by means

which may communicate to another the greatest of blessings." [15]

A week later, the Rev. Gurley wrote again to Madison proposing that the Society try to raise money in England and France. Madison's reply reads in part:

"A vital object of the Institution (Colonization Society) being to free our country of a great internal evil, justice requires this; and our pride, while we are describing the prosperity of our country as greater than that of any other, would seem to be a motive against taxing any other for an interest so far as it may not be a common one." [16]

Only four days after having been elected President of the society, he said in a letter to Professor Dew, a violent opponent of abolition: "In my estimate of the experiment instituted by the Colonization Society, I may indulge too much my wishes and hopes, to be safe from error. But a partial success will have its value, and an entire failure will leave behind a consciousness of the laudable intentions with which relief from the greatest of our calamities was attempted in the only mode presenting a chance of effecting it." [17]

## IX.

### His Views in Old Age

As we have seen, Madison held no high opinion of the Negroes. In this respect he did not vary much from Jefferson's views. Perhaps his Southern environment had something to do with it, nevertheless, as he approached extreme old age he seems to have been more conscious of the moral evils of slavery and to have laid aside somewhat his strictly legal manner for one of more human sympathy and understanding. With reference to the approaching convention of the state of Virginia in which the question of the ratio of representatives in the two branches of the legislature was to be debated, he said:

"With respect to the slaves, they cannot be admitted as persons into the representation, and probably will not be allowed any claim as privileged property. As the difficulties and disquietudes on that subject arise mainly from the great inequality of slaves in the geographical division of the country, it is fortunate that the cause will abate as they become more diffused, which is already taking place; transfers of them from the quarters where they abound, to those where laborers are more wanted, being a matter of course." [1]

When the aged statesman addressed the convention later, he said in behalf of the colored population, "...It is due to justice; due to humanity; due to truth; to the sympathies of our natures; in fine to our character as a people, both abroad and at home, that they (slaves) should be considered, as much as possible, in the light of human beings, and not as mere property. As such, they are acted upon by our laws, and have an interest in our laws. They may be considered as making a part, though a degraded part, of the families to which they belong... the mere circumstance of complexion cannot deprive them of the character of men." [2]

As to the question of the ratio of representation in the two branches of the Virginia legislature, Madison recommends "the Federal number" (i.e., that five Negroes should count as three white men) "by its

simplicity, its certainty, its stability, and its perman-
ency, and also because . . . it is in conformity to the
ratio recognized in the Federal Constitution." [3]

In a letter dated January 8, 1830, in Richmond,
Madison further explains the above quotations.
"The technical cause of our difficulties has been the
colored population, which happens to lie in one
geographical half of the state, and to have been the
great object of taxation." [4]

Toward the end, Madison seems to have had a
premonition of the danger with which the problem
of slavery threatened the Union. In a letter dated
July 27, 1831, he said, "If the states cannot live
together in harmony under the auspices of such a
government as exists, and in the midst of blessings
such as have been the fruits of it, what is the prospect
threatened by the abolition of a common Government, with all the rivalships, collisions, and ani-
mosities inseparable from such an event?" And, he
proves no poor prophet when he adds, ". . . a protection of fugitive slaves substituted for the obligatory
surrender of them, would, of themselves, quickly
kindle the passions which are the forerunners of
war." [5]

Madison's last word on slavery is to be found in
a letter to Henry Clay written in June, 1833. "It is
painful to observe the unceasing efforts to alarm
the South by imputations against the North of
unconstitutional designs on the subject of the slaves.
You are right, I have no doubt, in believing that no
such intermeddling disposition exists in the body of
our Northern brethren. Their good faith is sufficiently
guaranteed by the interest they have as merchants,
ship-owners, and as manufacturers, in preserving a
union with the slaveholding states. On the other

hand, what madness in the South to look for greater
safety in disunion.... The danger from the alarm is,
that the pride and resentment exerted by them may
be an overmatch for the dictates of prudence, and
favor the project of a Southern Convention, insidi-
ously revived, as promising, by its councils, the best
securities against grievances of every sort from the
North." [4]

## X.

### Summary of Madison's Views

Madison was born into a slaveholding Virginian
family and was reared in much the same environment
as was Washington and Jefferson. As a young man
of thirty-four, he expressed the desire "to depend as
little as possible upon the labor of slaves." In the
debates in the Constitutional Convention of 1787,
he protested against the extension of the slave-trade
until 1808 as being "more dishonorable to the American character" than the failure to mention the word
"slaves" in the constitution. When, in 1808, the
slave trade was legally ended by the Act of 1807,
Madison noted that the importation of Negroes was
still secretly being conducted. Accordingly, when
he became President, he urged Congress to suppress
"this criminal conduct." Again, in 1816 he presented
the subject to Congress in a message, "... with a full
assurance of their disposition to apply all the remedy
which can be afforded by an amendment of the law."
He had a well-thought-out plan of freeing the
Negroes. Emancipation should be gradual and should
be with the consent of both the master and slave. He
held the view that the blacks and whites would never
be able to live at peace with one another, the reason

being that their physical differences would prove a constant source of irritation and contempt. While he held no brief for the good qualities of Negro character, he admitted that ". . . the mere circumstance of complexion could not deprive them of the character of men." He believed always that the real problem of emancipation was that of finding the proper asylum for those set free, and in his choice of places he recommended the Western territories in preference to Africa. In this point he never fully agreed with the Colonization Society although accepting its presidency in later life. He worked out the financial details for removing and freeing the Negroes but recognized that "all sorts of difficulties would be encountered."

At the time of the "Missouri question," he held the opinion that it was a mistake to prohibit Negroes from the states west of the Mississippi River, because he believed that the "diffusion" of the slaves in the land tended to meliorate their actual condition and to facilitate their eventual emancipation.

He was somewhat sensitive of the opinion of foreign countries as to the glaring inconsistency of the existence of slavery in a land founded on the principle that all men are created free and equal, and was anxious to bring about ". . . a rapid erasure of the blot from our Republican character."

He realized the danger of splitting the nation into parties based upon geographical instead of political distinctions, and asks ". . . what is to control those great repulsive masses from awful shocks against each other?" In this realization he seems to have had a premonition of the great Civil War that was to follow.

While there can be no doubt that Madison abhorred slavery and wished to see it ended, nevertheless, he appears rather cold and objective in his diagnosis of slavery problems and lacking in human feeling for the Negroes themselves. As late as 1829 he wrote that the slaves "... cannot be admitted as *persons* into the representation, and probably will not be allowed any claim as privileged property." His opinion of the Negroes was not very high, as, for example, when he wrote that they "... may be considered as making a part, though a degraded part, of the families to which they belong." Madison's viewpoint remained always influenced by his Southern environment. He appears to have been moved far more by the fact that slavery was not economically and politically sound, than by any purely moral motive, or desire to better the condition of the slaves. Nevertheless, he gave much thought to Negro problems and seems to have been conscious of "... the dreadful fruitfulness of the original sin of the African trade," at a time, when the majority of his countrymen were blind to the great danger inherent in the institution.

# Some Conclusions

Drawn From A Study Of The Foregoing Material

This study of the views of the leading men at the time of the Revolution and shortly after shows conclusively that they were all concerned with three main problems; how to stop the slave-trade; how to abolish slavery itself, and what should be done with the slaves, when once freed. Then, problems grew out of the attitude of the early colonists and their European proprietors, who thought that the great natural resources of America were meant to be consumed and exploited as quickly and ruthlessly as possible. The English manufacturers realized that the slave trade, which began in the reign of Queen Elizabeth, was a great stimulant to American agriculture and would furnish raw materials for their mills. On the other hand, the presence of the English markets and their ability to absorb all the raw materials that were produced, proved a stimulant to the plantation owners to increase their laborers. And while it is true, as Jefferson claimed that the slave trade was imposed upon the colonists by powers outside of the colonies, it is also true that the colonists too quickly forgot their scruples against it. Any student of the period must admit that with the occasional outbursts of honest indignation against slavery and the slave trade there existed a great deal of moral indifference and unconcern which allowed this great social problem to develop.

The attempts to solve it can be divided into three

165

recognizable elements: the moral, political, and economic. The early efforts of the Quakers, and those of
Benjamin Franklin and the Pennsylvania Abolition
Society, are excellent examples of attempts to make
the nation conscious of the moral evils of slavery, but
they all failed to overcome the moral indifference of
those who were profiting from the institution. There
were times, such as during the Federal Convention
of 1787, or while the Act of 1807 was being debated,
that a concentrated moral effort might have succeeded, but this was defeated by the inclination to make
political bargains. While it is true that the slave
trade was *legally* abolished by the Act of 1807, it is
not true that it was actually abolished, and the institution of slavery itself was allowed to remain. In
fact, after 1807, all hope for the success of the purely
moral efforts, was lost. Besides the moral indifference
to the censure of the civilized world as well as the
indifference to the necessity of enforcing its own laws
against violations of the slave trade, there were in fact
two opposing moralities, both loudly proclaimed from
the pulpits of the North and South, and both equally
well founded in scripture.[1] When the moral leadership
is itself divided, the case for authority comes under
suspicion and is weakened.[2]

The attempt to solve this social problem politically,
i.e., legally, was also a failure. All of the men, with
the exception of John Adams, whose opinions we
have examined, expressed the hope, if not the belief,
that the problem would be solved by legal means.
They were all mistaken. This shows the danger, and
falsity, of the view that everything the constitutional
fathers did was right. They made mistakes aplenty,
although, taken as a whole, they were men of good
education and ability. Many of the laws which were

passed in the early days of the republic were stimulated primarily by the fear of a Negro insurrection, or a desire to justify to the civilized world the glaring incongruity of legal slavery existing in a land which boasted that "all men are created equal."

The economic attempts at solution had, from the beginning, the best chance of success although they were the least tried. We have seen that both Jefferson and Madison advised the gradual replacement of Negro by white labor. Among the economic attempts at solution, were the frequent efforts to prohibit the immigration of Negroes by fixing high tariffs. There was, as well, the work of various charitable and state organizations to restore the economic balance caused by slavery, by trying to better the condition of the Negroes so that they would be able to bear the responsibilities of freemen. While these efforts were not purely economic in nature, they were sustained by the powerful motive of material gain which would follow when the slaves gave place to free labor. The utter hopelessness of making money on large slave-holding plantations, which condition nearly ruined Washington, Jefferson and Madison, was another economic motive for a change.

Looking back on these efforts of early America to meet and solve this great social problem, it is easy for us to point out what ought and ought not to have been done. There is one great lesson which we can learn from a study of this period. This is: that moral problems of this nature must be faced and met as early as possible; postponement is not solution, and political bargains and compromises merely postpone problems to be dealt with by future generations.

# Notes

## PART I

**Chapter II:**

1 Jared Sparks, *The Works of Benjamin Franklin*, Vol. I, pp. 314, 315.

2 *Ibid*, Vol. VII, pp. 201, 202.

3 *Ibid*.

4 *Ibid*, Vol. IV, p. 70.

5 *Ibid*, Vol. VIII, pp. 16, 17.

6 *Ibid*, p. 42.

7 *Ibid*, Vol. X, p. 119.

**Chapter III:**

1 Dr. Richard Price, a nonconforming minister and political radical, published a pamphlet in 1776, entitled *Observation on Civil Liberty and the Justice and Policy of the War in America*, in which he espoused America's side in the controversy with the mother country. During the Revolution he was invited to come to the United States and become a citizen in order to help them with their finances. This he declined on account of age and of not feeling qualified.

In 1780, during the Revolution, Franklin wrote Price, consoling him on the abuse his writings had met with and predicting that they would come eventually into high esteem. (Sparks, *The Works of Benjamin Franklin*, Vol. III, p. 417.)

In a later letter we find Franklin sending his respects to a club at a London coffee house of which Dr. Price and Priestley were both members. He recognized that Dr. Price had done everything in his power to avoid the war between America and England. He says again of Dr. Price's pamphlet on liberty, ". . . It was a good one and will do good." (*Ibid*, Vol. X, p. 113.) We learn also in this letter that Dr. Price held Deist views in religion with which Franklin was in sympathy.

2 He refers to what was then taking place in Holland, Brabant and in France.

3 Sparks, *The Works of Benjamin Franklin*, Vol. X, pp. 320, 321.

4 *Ibid*, pp. 513, 514.
5 *Ibid*, p. 403.

Chapter IV:

1 *Annals of Congress*, Vol. II, p. 119f.
2 Henry Wilson, *History of the Rise and Fall of the Slave Power in America*, Vol. I, p. 61.
3 *Ibid*, p. 62. Doubtless confused with St. Paul.
4 *Ibid*, p. 63.
5 *Ibid*, p. 64.
6 *Annals of Congress*, Vol. I, 11, p. 1197.
7 Sparks, *The Works of Benjamin Franklin*, Vol. II, pp. 517-527.

## PART II

Chapter II:

1 Executive journals of the Council of Virginia I, 86 and I, 317. Lodge gives a good account of the institution of slavery in Virginia in his *A Short History of the English Colonies in America*, p. 68.
2 H. A. Washington, *The Writings of Thomas Jefferson*, Vol. VIII, p. 403.
3 Albert Jay Nock, *Jefferson*, p. 212.
4 Worthington Chauncy Ford, *Washington as an Employer and Importer of Labor*, p. 10.
5 Paul Leland Haworth, *George Washington, Country Gentleman*, p. 193.
6 John Fitzpatrick, ed., *The Diaries of George Washington*, Vol. I, pp. 118-120.
7 *Ibid*, Vol. I, p. 121.
8 Ford, *op. cit.*, p. 29.
9 Worthington Chauncy Ford, ed.: *The Writings of George Washington*, Vol. XII, p. 240.
10 Ford, *Washington as an Employer . . .*, p. 43.
11 Ford, *The Writings of George Washington*, Vol. II, p. 211-212.
12 The legislative body of Virginia, in fact the first legislative body set up on the North American continent.
13 *Washington, the Proprietor of Mt. Vernon*, U.S. George Washington Bicentennial Commission. No. 9, 5.

Chapter III:

1 John Fitzpatrick, ed., *The Diaries of George Washington*, Vol. I, p. 278.
2 *Ibid*, p. 383.
3 Haworth, *George Washington, Country Gentleman*, p. 192.

4 Virginia Historical Society, *Collection* . . ., Vol. VI, Preface Note 13.

5 *Washington, the Colonial and National Statesman*, U.S. George Washington Bicentennial Commission. No. 6, p. 2.

6 Virginia Historical Society, *Collection* . . ., Vol. VI, Preface Note 14, citing Journal of the House of Burgesses, p. 131.

7 Ford, *Washington as an Employer* . . ., p. 10.

8 Sparks, ed., *The Writings* of George Washington, Vol. II, pp. 494, 495.

9 Philip Alexander Bruce, *Economic History of Virginia in the Seventeenth Century*, Vol. II, p. 93.

10 Virginia Historical Society, *Collection* . . ., Vol. III, Preface Note 11.

11 *Ibid*, 12.

12 Thomas Jefferson belonged to this small class.


Chapter IV:

1 George Livermore, *An Historical Research respecting the Opinions of the Founding Fathers of the Republic on Negroes as Slaves, as Citizens and as Soldiers*, p. 93.

2 *American Archives*, ed. by Peter Force. Fourth Series, Vol. II, p. 762.

3 George Bancroft, *History of the United States*, Vol. VII, p. 421.

4 Livermore, *op. cit.*, pp. 115, 117.

5 *American Archives*, Fourth Series, Vol. II, p. 1630.

6 *Ibid*, Vol. III, p. 1385.

7 William Reed, *Life and Correspondence of President Reed*, Vol. I, p. 135.

8 Sparks, ed., *The Writings of George Washington*, Vol. III, p. 212.

9 *Ibid*, p. 218.

10 *Journals of the Continental Congress*, Vol. IV, p. 60.

11 "Schloezer's Briefwechsel," quoted from Livermore's *Historical Research* . . ., p. 111.


Chapter V:

1 *Pennsylvania Magazine*, April 1776, p. 193.

2 Ford, ed., *The Writings of George Washington*, Vol. III, p. 442.

3 Reed, *op. cit.*, Vol. I, p. 159.

4 Ford, *Writings of Washington*, Vol. III, p. 440. Also Sparks, *Writings of Washington*, Vol. III, p. 297.

5 Knapp, *Memoirs of Phillis Wheatley*, p. 36.

6 Benson John Lossing, *Field Book of the Revolution*, Vol. I, p. 556.

Chapter VI:

1 H. A. Washington, *The Writings of Thomas Jefferson*, Vol. I, pp. 23, 24.

2 *Ibid*, p. 19.

3 Varick Transcripts, p. 214.

4 "Washington's Letters to Governors," Varick Transcripts, p. 214. Washington had written to all Governors to recruit their forces to full strength on December 29, 1777.

5 Ford, ed., *Writings of Washington*, Vol. VI, p. 349.

Chapter VII:

1 *Memoirs of Colonel John Laurens*, p. 108.

2 Ford, *Writings of Washington*, Vol. VI, p. 348.

3 John C. Hamilton, ed., *The Works of Alexander Hamilton*, Vol. I, pp. 76-77.

4 Ford, ed., *Writings of Washington*, Vol. VII, p. 371.

5 *Ibid*.

6 Livermore, *Historical Research*, p. 119.

7 Hamilton, *Works of Hamilton*, Vol. I, p. 214.

8 Sparks, *Writings of Washington*, Vol. VIII, p. 323.

9 *Ibid*, p. 322.

Chapter VIII:

1 *Correspondence of the American Revolution*, Vol. III, p. 547.

2 Ford, *Writings of Washington*, Vol. X, p. 220

3 Livermore, *Historical Research*, p. 151.

4 Sparks, *Writings of Washington*, Vol. VIII, p. 431.

5 Ford, *Writings of Washington*, Vol. IX, p. 247.

6 Sparks, *Writings of Washington*, Vol. VIII, p. 439.

7 Owen Wister, *The Seven Ages of Washington*, p. 195.

8 *The Works of John Adams*, Vol. VIII, p. 376.

9 Sparks, *Writings of Washington*, Vol. IX, pp. 163, 164.

10 Livermore, *Historical Research*, p. 32.

Chapter IX:

1 Fitzpatrick, *The Diaries of Washington*, Vol. II, p. 379.

2 *Ibid*.

3 *Ibid*, Vol. III, p. 22.

4 Ford, *Writings of Washington*, Vol. XI, p. 25.

5 *Ibid*, p. 62.

6 Washington's Letter Book, 6A, p. 208. (Congressional Library)

7 *Ibid*, 6B, p. 6.

Chapter X:

1 See: John Fiske, *The Critical Period of American History*, chapters VI and VII.

2 Sparks, *Writings of Washington*, Vol. I, p. 436.

Chapter XI:

1 Sparks, *Writings of Washington*, Vol. X, p. 85.
2 *Annals of Congress*, Vol. I, 11 p. 1197.
3 *Debates in Congress* (Abridgement), Vol. I, p. 207 et seq.
4 Fitzpatrick, *Diaries of Washington*, Vol. IV, p. 103.
5 Sparks, *Writings of Washington*, Vol. X, p. 82.
6 Haworth, *George Washington, Country Gentleman*, p. 216.
7 *Ibid*, p. 214.
8 *Ibid*, p. 221.
9 Washington, "Farewell Address."
10 Sparks, *Writings of Washington*, Vol. XII, p. 323.

Chapter XII:

1 Washington Irving, *Life of George Washington*, p. 764 (One volume edition).
2 Ford, *Writings of Washington*, Vol. XIV, p. 196.
3 Haworth, *George Washington, Country Gentleman*, p. 217.
4 Sparks, *Writings of Washington*, Vol. XII, p. 569-670.

PART III

1 Charles Francis Adams, *The Works of John Adams*, Vol. X, p. 380.

PART IV

Chapter II:

1 Autobiography in H. A. Washington, *The Writings of Thomas Jefferson*, Vol. I, p. 1.
2 *Ibid*.
3 *Ibid*, Vol. I, p. 2.
4 Albert Jay Nock, *Jefferson*, p. 5.
5 *The Writings of Thomas Jefferson*, Vol. I, p. 2.
6 *Ibid*, p. 3.
7 *Ibid*.

Chapter III:

1 *Ibid*.

Chapter IV:

1 *Ibid*, p. 7.

2 *Ibid*, p. 8.
3 *Ibid*, pp. 8, 9.
4 *Ibid*, p. 8.
5 *Ibid*, p. 135.

Chapter V:

1 See: *Die amerikanische Revolutionsidee*, by Otto Vossler, p. 49.
2 *Declaration of Independence*, italico mine.
3 From a letter to Clark Sheldon, December 5, 1825.
4 *The Writings of Thomas Jefferson*, Vol. VII, p. 407.
5 Vossler, *Amerikanische Revolutionsidee*, p. 83.
6 John Locke, *Of Civil Government*, Book II.
7 Gilbert Chinard, *The Commonplace Book of Thomas Jefferson*, p. 73.
8 See: Carl Becker, *The Declaration of Independence*.
9 Francis Hirst, *Life and Letters of Thomas Jefferson*, p. 127, 128.
10 Clause struck out of the Declaration of Independence.
11 *The Writings of Thomas Jefferson*, Vol. I, p. 19.
12 *Ibid*, Vol. VIII, p. 500.

Chapter VI:

1 *Ibid*, Vol. I, pp. 58, 59.
2 i.e., the Church of England.
3 This was written in 1821.
4 Proposed in 1776 and finally carried in 1779.

Chapter VII:

1 *The Notes of Virginia*, first privately printed, Paris 1784.
2 For a history of this publication see P. L. Ford, *The Writings of Thomas Jefferson*.
3 Memorial Edition, Vol. V, p. 3.
4 All unmarked quotations in this chapter are to be found in "Notes of Virginia" in: H. A. Washington, *The Writings of Thomas Jefferson*, Vol. III, pp. 379-378.
5 See page 44 of this book.
6 Cato, *De Re Rustica*, c. 2.
7 *The Writings of Thomas Jefferson*, Vol. V, p. 429.
8 Query XVIII.
9 *The Writings of Thomas Jefferson*, Vol. II, p. 357.

Chapter VIII:

1 Typhoid fever.
2 Letter to Dr. Gordon, dated 1788; *Writings of Jefferson*, Vol. II, pp. 426, 427.

3 See page 134 of this book.
4 *Writings of Jefferson*, Vol. II, p. 427.
5 Thomas Jefferson's "Farm Book", p. 67.
6 *Ibid.*
7 *Ibid.*
8 *Ibid.*
9 Nock, *Jefferson*, p. 68.


Chapter IX:
    1 Hirst, *Life and Letters of Thomas Jefferson*, p. 524.
    2 *House Journal* (reprinted, 1826), 9th Congress, 2nd. sess.,
V. 468.
    3 *Annals of Congress*, 9th Congress, 2nd. sess., p. 1267.
    4 cf. Act of 1807.
    5 cf. Act of 1807.
    6 Statutes at Large, II., 426.
    7 December 10, 1819.
    8 *Writings of Jefferson*, Vol. VII, p. 200.


Chapter X:
    1 *Ibid*, Vol. IX, pp. 514-515.

## PART V

Chapter I:
    1 *Letters and Other Writings of James Madison*, Vol., p. 161.
    2 *Ibid*, pp. 217, 218 (Jan. 22, 1786).


Chapter II:
    1 Elliot, *Debates*, V. p. 477.
    2 *Ibid.*
    3 *Madison's Writings*, Vol. IV, p. 60.
    4 *Ibid*, Vol. III, p. 150.
    5 *Madison's Writings*, Vol. I, p. 322.
    6 Jan. 22, 1788.
    7 These articles were later printed under the title of *The Federalist*. The quotation is to be found under No. XLII.
    8 *Madison's Writings*, Vol. IV, p. 188.
    9 *Ibid*, Vol. I, p. 542.


Chapter III:
    1 Georgia, South Carolina and North Carolina.
    2 *House Journal*, 11th Congress, 3rd sess., VII, 435.
    3 *Ibid*, 14th Congress, 2nd sess., pp. 15-16.

Chapter IV:

  1 *Encyclopaedia Britannica*, article on Madison.
  2 *Madison's Writings*, Vol. III, p. 133.
  3 *Ibid*, p. 134.
  4 *Ibid*.
  5 *Ibid*, p. 135.
  6 *Ibid*.
  7 Ibid.
  8 *Ibid*, pp. 135-136.
  9 *Ibid*, p. 170.


Chapter V:

  1 *Ibid*, Vol. III, pp. 239, 240.
  2 *Ibid*, pp. 495-498.
  3 *Ibid*, pp. 541, 542.
  4 *The Pro-Slavery Argument*. Philadelphia, 1853.
  5 *The Restrictive System* and *The Slave Question*.
  6 *Madison's Writings*, Vol. IV, p. 274. Letter to Thomas Dew,
Feb. 23, 1833.
  7 *Ibid*, p. 277.


Chapter VI:

  1 *Madison's Writings*, Vol. III, pp. 310-315.
  2 *Ibid*, pp. 121, 122.


Chapter VII:

  1 *Ibid*, pp. 149-157.
  2 *Ibid*, pp. 164-165.
  3 In the Constitution of the United States, Art. IV, Sec. III,
Clause 2, Congress is given . . . "the power to dispose of and make
all needful rules and regulations respecting the territory or other
property belonging to the United States . . ."
  4 *Madison's Writings*, Vol. III, pp. 168, 169.
  5 *Ibid*, pp. 190-191.
  6 *Ibid*, p. 199.


Chapter VIII:

  1 Henry Wilson, *History of the Rise and Fall of the Slave
Power in America*, Vol. I, chap. XV.
  2 *Ibid*, chap. XV, p. 212.
  3 *Ibid*.
  5 *Ibid*, Vol. I, p. 218.
  6 *Ibid*, p. 214.
  7 Statement attributed to Daniel Webster.
  8 Wilson, *op. cited*, Vol. I, p. 220.

9 See page 136 of this book.
10 *Madison's Writings*, Vol. III, p. 135.
11 *Ibid*, p. 193.
12 *Ibid*, p. 240.
13 *Ibid*, Vol. IV, p. 60.
14 *Ibid*, pp. 213, 214.
15 *Ibid*, p. 274.
16 *Ibid*.
17 *Ibid*, p. 277.

Chapter IX:

1 *Ibid*, pp. 2-3.
2 *Ibid*, pp. 52, 53.
3 *Ibid*, p. 53.
4 *Ibid*, p. 57.
5 *Ibid*, p. 199.
6 *Ibid*, p. 307.

## CONCLUSIONS

1 See: Prof. Dew's article in *The Pro-Slavery Argument*, Philadelphia, 1853, pp. 451-461. Also: I Corinth. VII, 20, 21; I Tim. VI, i, 2; I Peter, II, 18, 20; Titus, II, 9, 10; Ephesians, VI, 5; Philemon, III, 22 and Colossians, IV, 1.

2 See: Van der Velde, *The Presbyterian Churches and the Federal Union*, 1868-1869, Harvard, 1932.

# Bibliography

Adams, Charles Francis: *The Works of John Adams, Second President of the United States.* 10 vols. Boston, 1850-1856.

Bancroft, George: *A History of the United States.* 10 vols. 1834-74.

Beard, Charles: *Economic Origins of Jeffersonian Democracy.* New York, 1927.

Becker, Carl: *The Declaration of Independence: A Study in the History of Political Ideas.* New York, 1922.

Blankenship, Russel: *American Literature as an Expression of the National Mind.* New York, 1931.

Bowers, Claude: *Jefferson and Hamilton: The Struggle for Democracy in America.* Boston and New York, 1925.

Bruce, Philip Alexander: *Economic History of Virginia in the Seventeenth Century.* 2 vols. New York and London, 1895.

Cairns, J.E.: *The Slave Power,* London, 1862.

Chinard, Gilbert, ed.: *The Commonplace Book of Thomas Jefferson: A Repertory of his Ideas on Government.* Baltimore and Paris, 1926.

Chinard, Gilbert: *Thomas Jefferson, Apostle of Americanism.* Boston, 1929.

Dew, Thomas R.: *Lectures on the Restrictive System.* Richmond, 1849.

Dew, Thomas R.: *The Slave Question,* n.d.

Dew, Thomas R.: "Review of the Debate in the Virginia Legislature of 1831 and 1832," in *The Pro-Slavery Argument.* Philadelphia, 1853.

Dodd, William: *Statesmen of the Old South; or from Radicalism to Conservative Revolt.* New York, 1912.

Donnan, Elizabeth, ed.: *Documents Illustrative of the History of the Slave Trade to America.* 4 vols. Washington, D.C., 1930-35.

DuBois, W.E.B.: *The Suppression of the African Slave Trade to the United States of America: 1638-1870.* New York, 1896.

Elliot, Jonathan, ed.: *The Debates in the Several State Conventions on the Adoption of the Federal Constitution.* 5 vols. Washington, D.C., 1836-1845.

Fiske, John: *The Critical Period of American History, 1783-1789.* Boston, New York and Cambridge, 1898.

179

Fiske, John: Essays, Historical and Literary. 2 vols. New York and
    London, 1902.
Fitzpatrick, John, ed.: The Diaries of George Washington, 1748-
    1799. 4 vols. Boston, 1925.
Ford, Paul Leicester: The Writings of Thomas Jefferson. 10 vols.
    New York, 1892-1899.
Ford, Worthington Chauncy: Washington as an Employer and
    Importer of Labor, Brooklyn, N.Y., 1889.
Ford, Worthington Chauncy, ed.: The Writings of George Wash-
    ington. 14 vols. New York and London, 1889-1893.
Hamilton, John C., ed.: The Works of Alexander Hamilton. 7 vols.
    New York, 1850-1851.
Haworth, Paul Leland: George Washington, Country Gentleman.
    Indianapolis, 1925.
Hirst, Francis: Life and Letters of Thomas Jefferson. New York,
    1926.
Irving, Washington: Life of George Washington. 5 vols. New York,
    1855-1859.
Knapp: Memoirs of Phyllis Wheatley, 1807.
Laurens: Memoirs of Colonel John Laurens. 1808.
Livermore, George: An Historical Research respecting the Opinions
    of the Founding Fathers of the Republic on Negroes as
    Slaves, as Citizens and as Soldiers. Boston, 1863.
Locke, John: Of Civil Government. New York, 1890.
Lodge, Henry Cabot: A Short History of the English Colonies in
    America. New York, 1881.
Lodge, Henry Cabot, ed.: The Federalist: A Commentary on the
    Constitution of the United States. New York, 1888.
Lossing, Benson John: The Pictorial Field Book of the Revolution.
    2 vols. New York, 1851-1852, 1859-1860 and 1860.
Macy, Jesse: The Anti-Slavery Crusade: A Chronicle of the Gather-
    ing Storm. New Haven, 1919.
Mazyck, Walter: George Washington and the Negro. Washington,
    D.C., 1932.
Nock, Albert Jay: Jefferson. New York, 1930.
Parrington, Vernon: Main Currents in American Thought: An In-
    terpretation of American Literature from the Beginning to
    1920. Vol. 1, 1620-1800: The Colonial Mind. 3 vols. in 1.
    New York, 1930.
Reed, William: Life and Correspondence of President Reed. Phila-
    delphia, 1797.
Russell, Phillips: Benjamin Franklin, the First Civilized American.
    New York, 1926.
Scudder, Horace Elisha: George Washington, an Historical Biogra-
    phy. Boston and New York, 1889.
Sparks, Jared: The Works of Benjamin Franklin. 10 vols. Chicago,
    1882.

Sparks, Jared: The Life of Benjamin Franklin, containing The Autobiography, with Notes and a Continuation. Boston, 1856.

Sparks, Jared, ed.: The Writings of George Washington. 12 vols. Boston, 1834-1837.

Stephen, James: West Indian Slavery in Law and Practice: The Slavery of the British West India Colonies Delineated. 2 vols. London, 1824-1830.

Tyler, Moses Coit: The Literary History of the American Revolution. 2 vols. New York and London, 1897.

Van der Velde, Lewis George: The Presbyterian Churches and the Federal Union, 1861-1869. Cambridge and London, 1932.

Vossler, Otto: Die amerikanischen Revolutionsideale in ihrem Verhältnis zu den europäischen, untersucht an Thomas Jefferson. Munich, 1929.

Washington, H.A.: The Writings of Thomas Jefferson. 9 vols. Washington, D.C., 1853-1854.

Weems, Mason Locke: A History of the Life and Death, Virtues and Exploits of George Washington. New York, 1927. First published 1800.

Wilson, Henry: History of the Rise and Fall of the Slave Power in America. 3 vols. Boston, 1878.

Wister, Owen: The Seven Ages Of Washington: A Biography. New York, 1910.

---

The following sources were also used:

American Archives. Edited by Peter Force. 3 vols. Washington, D.C., 1848-1853.

Annals of the Congress of the United States.

Correspondence of the American Revolution.

Journals of the Continental Congress.

Pennsylvania Magazine. Vol. 2 (April 1776).

United States George Washington Bicentennial Commission: Washington, the Proprietor of Mt. Vernon. Washington, D.C., 1932.

United States George Washington Bicentennial Commission: Washington, the Colonial and National Statesman. Washington, D.C., 1932.

Varick Transcripts.

Virginia Historical Society: Collections of the Virginia Historical Society. Richmond, 1833-1892.

Washington's Letter Book, Congressional Library.

U.S. Congress: *Abridgement of the Debates of Congress from 1789-1856.* Edited by Thomas Hart Benton. 16 vols. New York, 1857-1861.

United States House of Representatives. *Journals.*

*Letters and Other Writings of James Madison,* 4 vols. Published by order of Congress. Philadelphia, 1865.

*The Writings of Thomas Jefferson.* Andrew A. Lipscomb, editor in chief of the Thomas Jefferson Memorial Association of the United States. 20 vols. Washington, D.C., 1903-1904.

*Thomas Jefferson's Farm Book.* Unpublished manuscript in the possession of the Massachusetts Historical Society, with miscellaneous pages in the possession of the Alderman Library, the University of Virginia, and the collection of Roger Barrett in Chicago. (First published by the Princeton University Press for the American Philosophical Society in 1953. Ed. by Edwin Morris Betts.)

*Encyclopedia Britannica.* 14th edition. London and New York, 1929.

# Index

# New American Review 1 2 3 4

In its first year of publication, NAR has established itself as the bold new voice of American writing. Each issue of this paperback periodical contains more than 250 pages of fiction, essays, and poetry that speak to the issues of American experience here and now. NAR has been hailed as "the best of the literary journals" (*The Commonweal*) and as "a vital dialogue between public concern and private imagination." (*Book World*) Here are some of the reasons why:

NEW AMERICAN REVIEW #1
Fiction by William H. Gass, Grace Paley, Philip Roth; Stanley Kauffman on his experiences as drama critic for *The New York Times;* Richard Gilman on "MacBird and Its Audience," "Burke and Marx" by Conor Cruise O'Brien.                    (#Q3254—95¢)

NEW AMERICAN REVIEW #2
Fiction by Allen Friedman, E. L. Doctorow, Edward Hoagland, and John Barth; poetry by Günter Grass; essays by Nat Hentoff, Neil Compton and Staughton Lynd.                    (#Q3365—95¢)

NEW AMERICAN REVIEW #3
Featuring Philip Roth's "Civilization and Its Discontents." Other fiction by R. V. Cassill and Donald Barthelme; essays by Josephine Herbst, George Dennison, and Frank Kermode.
(#Y3455—$1.25)

NEW AMERICAN REVIEW #4
An emphasis on politics and political criticism featuring Robert Coover's "The Cat in the Hat for President." Other pieces by Eric Bentley, Conor Cruise O'Brien and Mordecai Richler.
(#Y3562—$1.25)

## why not
## subscribe to ...

# New American Review

## 5 6 7 8

As a subscriber, you will receive the next four issues of NEW AMERICAN REVIEW at the special price of $4.00 (regular price $5.00).

## A BONUS BOOK TO SUBSCRIBERS

We'll send you free either

NAR #1 ☐
NAR #2 ☐
NAR #3 ☐
NAR #4 ☐

that's in addition to your $1.00 savings as a NAR subscriber.

The New American Review
Subscription Department
1937 Williamsbridge Road
Bronx, New York 10461

I enclose my check for $4.00. Please send me the 4-issue subscription to New American Review. My subscription will begin with NAR #5.

NAME_____

ADDRESS_____

CITY_____STATE_____ZIP_____

You may also obtain the other NAR issues by enclosing the per issue price, plus 10¢ for handling and postage for each issue you want.

☐ NAR #1—$.95 . ☐ NAR #2—$.95 ☐ NAR #3—$1.25
☐ NAR #4—$1.25 (check one or more)

Offer good in U.S. and Canada only

## Other MENTOR Books of Special Interest

☐ **JEFFERSON (revised and abridged) by Saul K. Padover.** The story of Jefferson as farmer, philosopher, architect, statesman and President of the United States.
(#MT809—75¢)

☐ **DEMOCRACY IN AMERICA (abridged) by Alexis de Tocqueville.** The classic critique of freedom and democracy in 19th century America by a brilliant Frenchman.
(#MQ788—95¢)

☐ **A DOCUMENTARY HISTORY OF THE UNITED STATES (revised, expanded) edited by Richard D. Heffner.** Important documents that have shaped America's history, with commentary.
(#MT605—75¢)

☐ **AMERICA IN PERSPECTIVE edited by Henry Steele Commager.** Commentary on our national characteristics by 20 perceptive observers from Tocqueville to Brogan.
(#MT424—75¢)

---

**THE NEW AMERICAN LIBRARY, INC., P.O. Box 2310, Grand Central Station, New York, New York 10017**

Please send me the MENTOR BOOKS I have checked above. I am enclosing $_____(check or money order—no currency or C.O.D.'s). Please include the list price plus 10¢ a copy to cover mailing costs. (NEW YORK CITY residents add 5% Sales Tax. Other New York State residents add 2% plus any local sales or use taxes).

Name_____

Address_____

City_____State_____Zip Code_____

Allow at least 3 weeks for delivery